THE PASTA MACHINE COOKBOOK

Donna Rathmell German

BRISTOL PUBLISHING ENTERPRISES
San Leandro, California

A Nitty Gritty® Cookbook

Printed in the United States of America.

ISBN 1-55867-081-5

Cover design: Frank Paredes
Cover photography: John Benson
Food stylist: Suzanne Carreiro

CONTENTS

Rub a dub-dub
Three girls in the tub
And who do you think they be?
A butcher, a baker
and a pasta maker.
Turn them out, cooks all three.

This book is dedicated to my daughters,
Rachel (5), Katie (3) and Helen (2),
and to their huge appetite for pasta.

Many thanks to Alison Boleski and Rhonda Lechner
for their help in testing recipes.

HOMEMADE PASTA: EQUIPMENT, TECHNIQUES AND INGREDIENTS

Prior to the publication of this cookbook on pasta, pasta cookbooks were devoted almost entirely to sauces with which to serve the pasta. In contrast, this book explores the endless possibilities with the pasta itself. The most basic pasta is nothing more than flour and water, although egg is commonly used. With the recipes in this book, you can now make fresh, delicious, gourmet pastas at home. In addition to using fruits or vegetables to flavor the pasta itself, you can make flavorful herb pastas as well as pastas containing many grains and flours other than basic wheat.

Many of us live busy, hectic lifestyles these days. Pasta, even fresh, homemade pasta, makes a very quick, easy and nutritious meal. In many cases the sauce and the pasta may be started at the same time. If meat is being used and needs to marinate, it is easy make the marinade ahead of time and set it in the refrigerator until needed. Many of the recipes in this book are geared for very easy and fast preparation of meals.

An inexpensive, quick and highly nutritious meal, pasta is a favorite of people of all ages. Pasta itself is very healthy, low in fat (especially those recipes using no eggs or using nonfat yogurt) and high in carbohydrates. Meals with pasta help fill the USDA's recommendation to eat 6 or more servings of grains a day.

Nutritional Information

Pasta is an easy alternative to potatoes or rice with a meal. The following nutritional comparison is based on information in the U.S. Dept. of Agriculture's *Nutritive Value of Foods* brochure (*Home and Garden Bulletin Number 72*) and is for 1 cup of cooked, commercially made pasta (no egg or oil), 1 baked potato, 8 oz. with skin, and 1 cup cooked white rice.

	spaghetti	potato	rice
Calories	190	220	225
Protein, grams	7	5	4
Fat, grams	1	trace	trace
Carbohydrate, milligrams	39	51	50
Sodium, milligrams	1	16	0

The nutritional information in this book was compiled using *The Cooking Companion* and is for a 1-cup serving or a given fraction of the total recipe. The nutritional data is based on the largest number of servings for the sauces. Optional ingredients are not included in the comparison. If a range of ingredients is listed, the first or lower amount is selected.

About the Recipes

Unless otherwise noted, each of the recipes in this book makes approximately ½ lb. of pasta which serves approximately 2-3 as a main meal or 4-6 as a side dish. Each recipe may be easily doubled or tripled if desired. A pasta meal which is topped with a meatless sauce requires more pasta than one which is served with meat.

Dough consistency must vary according to whether you use a hand-crank pasta machine or an electric extruding pasta machine; two versions are given for most recipes.

In general, the dough should be kneaded for several minutes. Doughs which obtain moisture from vegetables or fruits may require longer kneading to evenly absorb and distribute the moisture throughout the dough. Don't be too quick to add water to these doughs, as you could end up with a dough which is too sticky. If this is the case, simply add 1 tablespoon of semolina flour at a time until the proper consistency is obtained. Recipes which must be monitored closely and those which require a good understanding for the proper consistency of the dough are marked *Advanced*.

It is very difficult to give precise measurements for pasta dough because there are so many variables, such as the size of the egg used, the humidity, the amount of moisture in the flour, and the flour itself. The dough made for use in a hand machine is more moist than that intended for an extruder. There are even slight differences in the texture required for each of the extruders, and I urge extruder owners to read the owner's manual for specifics on their machine. Making pasta is something that you have to develop a "feel" for, and may require some experimenting until you are comfortable with it. I urge you to start with a very basic semolina or herb recipe until you feel comfortable with how the dough should feel and look, and how to cut it. It is not difficult, but takes some getting used to.

USING A MANUAL MACHINE

Testing for hand-cranked pastas in this book was done using an Atlas (Marcato) pasta machine, sold under different names by various manufacturers and stores. There are many similar brands of hand-crank machines available at a reasonable price which operate in the same manner.

Making pasta using a hand-crank machine enables a wider variety of pasta to be made, for several reasons. Fruits and vegetables may be used more readily, as the main liquid for the dough and the appropriate puree will not clog, which it may do with the extruder dies. The addition of seeds such as caraway, anise or fennel is easily achieved without having to crush them first. Simply be careful not to roll the dough too thinly, as it may cause the seeds to tear the pasta. If the sheet of pasta does start to tear, stop rolling on the present setting and go back to the previous roller setting for your final roll.

Hand rolling and folding of the dough is thought by some to produce a better tasting, stronger dough. No dough is wasted, as every single piece may be easily passed through both the rollers and the cutters. Last, but not least, the cleanup of a hand cranked machine is as simple as wiping it dry with a towel; in fact, you do not want to wash the machine. I sometimes fold a paper towel and pass it through the rollers just to make sure I pick up all the moisture.

Kneading the Dough

The dough should be smooth, in one or two balls if using a machine to knead. Pasta dough is heavier and drier than a bread dough. Dough should be allowed to rest for 10 to 15 minutes after kneading and before rolling out. If cooking the pasta right away, this is a good time to start boiling the water and start making the sauce so that both will be ready at once. When using a machine to knead the dough, you may find that you need to add a tablespoon or two of water to help the dough form one or two balls. Be careful that the dough does not get too sticky as it will not roll out properly. Adding too much moisture is a common mistake. Lightly flour the dough before you set it aside to rest and then keep sprinkling the dough with a little flour during the rolling so it does not stick in the machine.

Using a bread machine: Place the ingredients into the baking pan as you would for a loaf of bread. Use the dough or regular white cycle and allow the machine to knead the dough for a half a minute or a minute — check the dough and adjust the flour or liquid if necessary to form a round ball of dough. Allow the machine to knead for approximately 5 minutes. Turn the machine off by using the stop or reset button.

Using a dough maker: Place the ingredients in the mixing chamber as usual. Allow the machine to knead the dough for approximately 5 minutes. After the first minute, check the consistency of the dough and adjust as necessary. Dough makers include machines which are specifically designed to mix yeast-leavened doughs or mixers which use dough hooks.

Using a food processor: Place the ingredients in the work bowl with the steel blade. Process for approximately 1 minute or until the dough starts to come together. Adjust the liquid or flour as necessary to form a round ball of dough. Allow the machine to knead the dough for another 2 to 3 minutes.

Kneading dough by hand: Place the dry ingredients on your kitchen counter and form a "well" in the center. Add liquid ingredients to the center of the flour and knead the dough together, scraping the flour from the outside into the liquid ingredients. Once the dough has formed a nice, smooth ball, continue to knead it by hand for several minutes.

Rolling the Dough

Passing the dough through the rollers serves to further knead the dough. Divide the dough in half and start rolling it through roller position #1, the widest. If the dough does not roll through smoothly or if it breaks, repeat the process using the same roller setting. This is particularly helpful during the first pass of the rollers. Some doughs may be difficult to pass through the first time and should be repeated until you obtain a nice smooth rectangle of dough, also called a sheet. The reason for this initial difficulty could be that the dough is somewhat dry, that it has not been kneaded sufficiently or that it has "rested" too long. Further kneading by passing through the rollers will help to soften it. I have passed a few doughs through the first roller up to ten times before I obtained a smooth sheet. Each time the dough is passed through the rollers on the widest setting, it should then be folded in thirds. This helps to knead the dough as well as to form the sheet into a nice, even rectangle.

Too sticky a sheet of pasta may stick to the rollers or even stick together after cutting. If the sheet of pasta feels the least bit sticky, it should be lightly floured between passes through the rollers. I often keep the kitchen counter floured and simply lay the sheet on top of the flour and then flip the dough so that the other side flours lightly. Of course, flour may be sprinkled lightly too — whichever way you find more convenient.

Once a smooth sheet of dough is obtained, it is no longer necessary to fold into thirds, although some people do. It may then be rolled through the next set of rollers, reducing the thickness of the rollers each time until the desired thickness is obtained. I generally roll to roller width 5 or 6 on the Atlas, which is the second or third width from the end. The thicker the pasta, the longer it takes to cook. It is not absolutely necessary to roll each roller width if the dough is rolling smoothly. For example, you could skip #3 and go right to #4. If the sheet of dough becomes too long to handle, simply cut it in half with a sharp knife, a pizza wheel or pastry cutter.

Roll the dough into sheets and allow to rest prior to cutting. You may hang the sheet over a wooden pasta rack, over a broom handle or even between two chairs.

As the process of rolling the dough takes a few minutes, by the time you finish rolling all the sheets out, it is probably time to start cutting the first strip.

Hand machines come with cutters for both fettuccine and spaghetti. Additional cutters which may be purchased include: angel hair, trenette, lasagna, varying thickness of spaghetti and even a ravioli press. If making lasagna, you may run the sheet through to your desired thickness and cut the sheet in half or thirds with a pizza wheel or sharp knife.

USING AN ELECTRIC EXTRUDER

An electric extruder mixes the dough in a special chamber and then pushes it out through a small metal or plastic disk called a die, which shapes the pasta. Extruder machines make various pasta shapes such as macaroni or ziti which may not be made in hand machines. Several different models of the machines mentioned later in this chapter are available with different dies.

The dry ingredients are placed in the mixing chamber of the machine and then the wet ingredients are added to it while the machine is mixing. If using ingredients for moisture such as spinach, you may add it with the dry ingredients — just spread it evenly on top of the flour.

It is imperative to follow manufacturer guidelines for the proper consistency of the dough for your particular machine. The general consistency of extruder pasta dough is much drier than the dough used with a hand machine. However, too dry a dough can jam the machine and may even cause damage. Too wet a dough will be sticky and could possibly break the die of the machine. The booklets which come with extruder machines contain very explicit pictures to indicate exactly what the dough should look like when ready to extrude. In order to prevent damage to your machine, I cannot emphasize enough the importance of following the manufacturer's guidelines in adjusting the dough.

If at any time your machine makes funny noises or sounds like it is struggling, stop the machine and start over. Do not continue, as it could seriously damage the machine.

Allow the machine to knead for several minutes and even a minute or two longer if using all semolina flour, which I recommend. I occasionally stop the machine and let the dough rest for a minute or two before extruding. However, during testing, I usually mixed the dough and then extruded it immediately.

Most manufacturers recommend soaking or rinsing the die in warm water just before the beginning of the extrusion process. Due to the hardness or high protein value of durum semolina, it may be slow to extrude initially, but as the dough continues to knead during the extrusion process, it becomes softer and quicker to extrude.

Extruder machines have difficulty with some doughs which use vegetable or fruit purees. In some cases, I did not include a recipe for the extruder because I had extreme difficulty in obtaining a good pasta from the machine.

Some doughs are worth making in the extruders but may be quite frustrating to work with and should not be attempted as your first try! These recipes are marked *Advanced*. An example is the spinach pasta. The kneading of the dough pulls the moisture from the spinach. If water is added too quickly, as the machine continues to knead and/or extrude, the liquid is still being pulled from the spinach and the last noodles will be nothing but soggy strands of green. This can make quite a mess in the extruder, which is then difficult to clean! This and similar recipes should be attempted after you have a good "feel" for your machine and the proper consistency of the dough.

If the pasta has uneven sides ("hairy"), it may mean the dough is too dry. This often occurs during the first few inches of extruded pasta and can be helped by rinsing or soaking the disk in warm water just before you begin the extruding process. As the pasta dough kneads and is pushed through the extrusion cavity, if often softens up and looses the "hairs." Similarly, tubular pasta such as ziti, rigatoni or macaroni which split indicate that the dough is too dry, and the consistency of the dough may require some adjustment.

Testing for this book was done using three different electric extruders (alphabetically):

- **Pasta Express x2000 by Creative Technologies Corp. (TAKKA)** - A 1½ lb. machine which comes with 11 dies including spaghetti, linguine, small and large macaroni/ziti, lasagna, bagel, vermicelli, fettuccine, pretzel or breadstick, gnocchi and cookie. A large macaroni/rigatoni die is available for additional purchase. The arm which kneads the dough reverses to extrude it. This feature enables the consistency of the dough to be corrected easily even after the start of extrusion. The same company sells two other machines: the x1000 comes with spaghetti, fettuccine, vermicelli, linguine, lasagna and small macaroni; the x3000 comes with all dies from the x2000 plus the large rigatoni. Too dry a dough may cause damage to the machine. Technical assistance is provided by calling 800-282-5240.

- **PastaMatic PMX700 by Simac** - A 1½ lb. machine which comes with 8 disks including thin and regular spaghetti, linguine, macaroni, fettuccine, cookies, lasagna and bucato. Flour or water is easily added to the mixing chamber to help adjust the consistency after extrusion begins. A shutter slide is opened or closed which controls whether the dough mixes or is pushed into the extrusion cavity. If dough is in the extrusion cavity, it must be extruded. The shutter may easily be closed, enabling the consistency of the remaining dough to be corrected. During testing I often ran recipe after recipe by starting the mixing of one dough after all the preceding dough had dropped into the extruder cavity. The first recipe would be extruding as the second was kneading. Trying to extrude dough which is too dry or wet may result in breaking the die and perhaps even the ring nut which holds the die in place. If the dough keeps going around but does not get pushed down into the extrusion cavity, it is too wet and should be broken into little pieces, flour added and mixed, and then pushed down into the hole. Simac also sells a 2½ lb. pasta machine, P1000, with the same 8 disks. Additional disks which may be ordered directly from the company include: large spaghetti, square spaghetti, small shells, farmer's pasta, medium or large fettuccine, hollow spaghetti, hollow ridged spaghetti, angel hair, square macaroni, ziti, pizza dough, bread sticks, gnocchi, clover macaroni or a wide width for ravioli. Technicians are available to answer questions about the machine: (800) 223-1898.

- **PastaPerfetto No. 900 by Vitantonio** - A 1 lb. machine which comes with 8 different disks including: thin, medium and large spaghetti, macaroni, fettuccine, lasagna, egg noodle and rigatoni. If the dough is too dry, the machine has a built-in mechanism which "clicks" to alert the user to turn it off, avoiding damage to the machine. If the extruding pasta becomes too wet as it's extruding (as can happen with the spinach pasta), the extruder knob may be turned and the remaining dough kneaded with some additional flour to obtain the correct consistency. Dough already in the extruder captivity will not be corrected and should not be placed back in the mixing chamber. A "Pasta Line" is available to answer questions about using the machine and any service/technical questions: (800) 837-1661.

SHAPING AND CUTTING THE PASTA

The ingredients remain the same for various pastas; the thicknesses and shapes may vary, making one recipe seem like several different ones. There are literally hundreds of various shapes and sizes of pastas made today, although Americans are most familiar with spaghetti, fettuccine and elbow macaroni. The shape of the pasta gives it characteristics which govern the type of sauce to serve with it.

The hand cranked machines make both fettuccine or spaghetti. The various pasta shapes which are easily made in the extruders include:

angel hair, fili d'oro, golden threads, capelli d'angeli - extremely fine spaghetti
capellini - thin spaghetti
vermicelli - medium spaghetti - "little strings"
spaghettoni - thick spaghetti
chitarre - square spaghetti
linguine - oval, thin strands, a cross between fettuccine and spaghetti
tagliatella - medium fettuccine
pappardella - large fettuccine
lasagna, sfoglia - wide ribbons varying in width from 1 to 2½ inches and layered
bucato, bucatino - tubular spaghetti
bucatino rigato - hollow ridged spaghetti - rigati is the term which means "ridged"
macaroni, maccherone - round, clover or square depending on machine or disk used
penne, ziti - tubular noodles which may be ridged or not. If 2 inches long, they may be called mostaccioli.
concigliette - small shells
pasta del Contadino - farmer's pasta, "S" shaped, short
rigati - means the tube has ridges

The following chart gives an idea of what type of sauce to serve with a particular shape or cut of pasta.

	cream	cheese	meat	tomato	oil/butter	soup	casserole
angel hair	no	no	no	yes	yes	yes	no
capellini	no	no	no	yes	yes	yes	no
spaghetti	unusual	yes	yes	yes	yes	yes	yes
linguine	yes	yes	yes	yes	yes	yes	no
fettuccine	yes	yes	yes	yes	yes	yes	no
lasagna	yes	yes	yes	yes	no	no	yes
bucato	yes	yes	yes	yes	yes	yes	yes
bucatino							
rigato	no	no	yes	yes	yes	yes	yes
macaroni	yes	yes	yes	yes	yes	yes	yes
penne/ziti	yes	yes	yes	yes	yes	yes	yes
small shells	yes	yes	yes	yes	yes	yes	yes

Making Ravioli

A single recipe from this book or ½ lb. of pasta makes about 2 dozen raviolis and uses about a cup of filling.

Hand crank machine with a ravioli attachment: Roll the dough into long, thin, even sheets. Fold the sheet in half and place the fold into the ravioli maker. Crank ever so slightly so that there is about ¼ inch sealed by the machine. Spread the sheet so that each half hangs over the side and place the filling between the two sheets. As the machine is cranked, the filling is sealed between the sheets of pasta and the raviolis are formed and cut. The ravioli attachment is available wherever pasta machines are sold.

Hand ravioli maker: Roll the dough into thin, even sheets just a little longer than the length of the ravioli maker. Lightly oil or spray the cutting plate and lay one of the sheets on top so that there is a slight overlap of dough on all four sides. Lightly oil or spray the forming plate and press it down on top of the dough so that pockets are formed. Fill the pockets and use a small pastry brush to brush a little water or milk around the edges of the flat area between the pockets. Place another sheet of pasta on top and use a rolling pin to both seal and cut the ravioli. Turn the plate over to lightly push the ravioli out. Hand ravioli makers are about the size and shape of an ice cube tray, are inexpensive, easy to use and may be found wherever pasta machines are sold.

By hand: Roll the dough into long, thin, even sheets. Place a sheet on a lightly floured counter top. Place filling in 1-teaspoon amounts on the sheet of pasta so that they are spaced about 2 inches apart with a ½-inch border between them. Using a small pastry brush, lightly brush milk or water between the fillings. Place a second sheet of pasta dough on top and press down on the sheets between the fillings to seal fillings in. Cut the ravioli with a sharp knife or pizza wheel. A special crimper and cutter may be used to seal and cut at the same time — available at kitchen or gourmet shops. Round raviolis may be made in much the same way. Half moon raviolis may be made by brushing a long sheet of pasta dough with milk or water and then cutting out circles. Place 1 teaspoon of filling on one side of the circle, leaving at least a 1/4-inch border. Close the other half over on top of it and seal closed by pressing firmly together. Note that if you shape the ravioli like this but also place your thumb in the center of the folded area and twist the ravioli around to form a circle around your thumb and seal, you've just made tortellini!

Extruder ravioli: Extrude the pasta through the lasagna die and proceed with the directions for making ravioli by hand.

Making Lasagna Noodles

A single recipe from this book or 1/2 lb. of pasta makes one 9x13-inch pan of lasagna with 3 to 4 layers of noodles.

By hand machine: You may purchase a special cutter for specific widths of lasagna noodles for your machine or you can simply roll the dough into long, thin, sheets and cut in half or thirds with a sharp knife or pizza wheel.

By extruder: Use the appropriate die for your machine.

As with any pasta which will be recooked, lasagna noodles should not be completely cooked, but removed from boiling water just before the al dente stage.

A typical lasagna casserole starts with a layer of tomato sauce (with or without vegetables or meat) followed by lasagna noodles, a cheese sauce and then tomato sauce again, repeating this sequence until the pan is full. The top layer usually has some kind of grated cheese on top and the casserole is then baked, uncovered, in a 375° oven for 30 to 40 minutes or a 350° oven for 40 to 50 minutes.

HINTS FOR HOME PASTA MAKING

Watch the dough for the proper consistency. Add a tablespoon of water if dough appears too dry and a tablespoon of flour if it appears too wet. Do this until the proper consistency is obtained. The amounts of liquid given were successful during testing; however, there are so many variables that you will learn by experience how to adjust the dough. There is a learning curve, but once you develop this "feel" for the dough, making pasta becomes second nature and you don't even think twice about what you are doing.

It is not necessary to dry the pasta prior to cooking it. Cut the pasta and put it directly into the boiling water or place it on the countertop until all is cut.

Freshly cut pasta may be dried by hanging for several hours (overnight), wrapped in plastic and refrigerated or frozen. I usually dry the pasta for approximately 12 hours on a wooden rack and then place it in an inexpensive plastic bag with a tie twist. This is nice for entertaining, as you can either make the pasta the day before or several hours before your guests arrive and hang the pasta to dry in the meantime. It is also fun to have a pasta party and have your guests help to roll and cut the pasta. Fresh pasta may be refrigerated in a sealed, airtight container for up to one week or frozen for up to one month. Do not thaw prior to cooking; simply drop the frozen pasta into the boiling water.

INGREDIENTS

Flour

Recipes in this book call for durum semolina, which is a coarsely milled (like cornmeal) flour from durum wheat, a very hard and high protein wheat used primarily for pasta making. Durum semolina may be found in many grocery stores, either with flour or with pasta; by mail order; or in gourmet kitchen or health food shops. If your grocery store does not carry it, ask the manager to order it for you. Durum flour may be found in some health food stores and is basically a whole wheat version of the semolina with a finer texture, similar to what most of us know as flour. Random testing was done using durum flour in place of semolina. It works very well and results in a nice brown colored pasta. If durum semolina or flour is unavailable, a good substitution would be bread flour which has a protein content somewhat lower than durum but still holds together nicely.

All purpose flour may be used, but it may result in dough which does not cut or shape as well. Using all purpose flour requires less water than semolina flour. Many recipes for pasta in other cookbooks recommend all purpose flour, but that is due mainly to the fact that until a few years ago only all purpose flour was readily available to the home pasta maker. Other flours used in these recipes are available in health food stores.

While semolina milled from durum wheat is very high in protein, it does lack some of the essential amino acids, as does any wheat product. By combining pasta (or any other wheat product) with other complementary proteins such as dairy products, beans and legumes, meat or seafood, a complete protein is formed. By combining some of these ingredients in the pasta itself, you are automatically providing one of the most nutritious pastas available. Examples of pastas containing complete protein are garbanzo or black bean, yogurt lemon pepper, sour cream, and buttermilk.

Oils

Vegetable, olive or walnut oils are included in most of the recipes and are really optional. When using the extruder machines, I found I liked the texture of the pasta better if I used oil. I have no preference for using oil with the hand machine and as a result, tend to omit it more often than not when cooking for my family. It is included in the recipes to give an idea of how much liquid is required for the recipes. If you choose to omit the oil, simply substitute water in its place and, as always, watch the dough for the proper consistency.

Eggs

Eggs are considered a normal ingredient in fresh pasta and should be fresh. Testing was done using either large or extra large eggs. Eggs are usually the main source of liquid ingredients for the dough. It may be necessary to adjust the liquid or flour depending on the egg used. If allergic to eggs, or if you simply prefer not to use them, you may substitute water. A general rule of thumb is that one egg equals ¼ cup of liquid; however, the size of eggs varies as does the way the egg is absorbed into the dough. The best method for substituting is to add the water slowly until the dough forms the proper consistency.

Fruits and Vegetables

If using fruits or vegetables (such as spinach) to contribute all or a large part of the liquid to the dough, allow the machine to mix or knead the dough for several minutes prior to adding water. Adding water too soon will result in a very sticky dough and pasta. As the dough is forced through the dies of the machine, the dough becomes moister and softer. If the dough becomes too sticky toward the end of extrusion or rolling, add a teaspoon or two of flour to the dough itself. Fruit or vegetable puree is made by placing the fruit or vegetable in a food processor with a steel blade or in a blender and processing until the fruit or vegetable is so finely chopped that it becomes a semi-liquid. Some vegetables such as broccoli or carrots require cooking prior to pureeing.

Seeds

Seeds such as caraway, anise, fennel, sesame, etc., can really spice up pasta, much like herbs and spices. If using an extruder, you may wish to crush them so that they do not clog the dies during extrusion. I use a mortar and pestle, but they could also be crushed in a zip lock bag with a rolling pin. Otherwise, I recommend using a die which has large holes so that there is less chance of clogging. For example, there is less chance of clogging a fettuccine die than an angel hair die. If using the hand machine, watch the dough carefully. If you notice that the dough is starting to tear around the seeds as you put it through the rollers, stop, go back to the previous width of rollers and make that your last roll.

Herbs and Spices

Herbs and spices in homemade pasta really make a difference compared to commercially prepared plain pasta. They make a flavorful side dish of pasta which only needs a little butter or olive oil tossed with it. The combinations of herbs and spices are endless. Please don't limit yourself to what I have listed in this book. Experiment with your favorite combinations and improvise. One thing that I noticed during testing was that fresh, chopped herbs worked wonderfully in pasta made in the hand machines. Unless the herbs are very finely chopped, there could be a clogging problem with the extruders. If substituting fresh, chopped herbs for dried herbs, a rule of thumb is to triple the amount. If you use the dried herbs as found in grocery stores, try crumbling them between your fingers to help bring out the flavor.

HINTS FOR COOKING AND SERVING PERFECT PASTA

- Use an adequately large pan. There are pans available at kitchen shops or department stores which are designed specifically for pasta cooking. While not necessary, these pans are nice as they have a stainless steel insert in which the pasta is cooked. The pasta is drained as the insert is lifted out of the water. Many of these pans also have a vegetable steamer which enables you to steam vegetables while the pasta is cooking!

- Use lots of boiling water. Most recipes in this book will result in approximately ½ lb. (8 oz.) of pasta which requires about 2 to 3 quarts of water. One full pound of pasta should be cooked in 4 to 6 quarts of water. If you are cooking vegetables to make the pasta (carrots or broccoli) or you are using them as part of the sauce, use the same water for boiling the pasta itself. In addition, you could use defatted chicken or beef stock, vegetable stock or bouillon cubes to impart a little extra flavor. A teaspoon or two of various herbs in the water, perhaps the same herbs as in the pasta, add flavor to the pasta.

- Add the pasta to the water slowly. Stir the pasta once it is in the water to prevent it from sticking together. This is extremely important if you have cut your pasta and then placed it on a plate or countertop or into a pasta insert prior to cooking. The water may be salted and/or oiled, a matter of preference. The oil decreases the foaming and prevents boiling over.

- Fresh pasta cooks in just minutes compared to commercially prepared dried pasta which generally cooks in 7 to 8 minutes. The thinner the pasta, the faster it cooks. The shape of the pasta itself may also affect cooking time, which means there are no hard and fast rules — just keep your eye on it.

- Pasta is done when *al dente*, which means it is tender or limp yet still firm to the bite. It usually rises to the top of the boiling water and floats. A pasta which is overcooked is very limp and soggy. I was also intrigued to note in the USDA's *Home and Garden Bulletin (#72) - Nutritive Value of Foods* that one cup of spaghetti cooked past the al dente stage to a "tender" (overcooked?) stage looses 2 grams of protein, 7 grams of carbohydrate, and 3 milligrams of calcium among other vitamin losses. Pasta which will be recooked in a casserole, such as lasagna, should be not be cooked completely; remove it from the heat just before the al dente stage.

- It is not necessary to rinse pasta after cooking as it could wash away some of the nutrients. If you wish to do so, however, make sure to use hot water so you will not cool the pasta. If the pasta is to be chilled or to be used in a casserole and baked again, it is customary to rinse it in cold water to stop the cooking and then toss it with butter or oil to prevent sticking prior to placing in the refrigerator to cool.

- Toss the cooked pasta with a little olive oil, butter or sauce immediately after cooking to prevent the strands from sticking together. Try warming the oil or butter in the bowl for a few seconds in the microwave so that your hot pasta goes right into a warmed bowl!

- Leftover, cooked pasta may be mixed with leftover sauce and refrigerated for a couple of days (2-3). It may be reheated on top of the stove or in the microwave for a minute or so.

- Leftover dough may be rolled into long strips (like a bread stick) and frozen for several hours. When well frozen, grate with a large-holed grater and use in soups or stews. These pasta pieces cook fairly quickly and should be added at the end of the cooking time.

GRAINS

BASIC SEMOLINA PASTA

This basic recipe is for any noodle product, as it contains egg.

	Hand	**Extruder**
durum semolina	1 cup	1⅓ cups
egg	1	1
vegetable or olive oil	1 tbs.	1 tbs.
water, if and as needed	1 tbs.	2 tbs.

per 1-cup serving   276 calories, 10.1 g protein, 42.2 g carbohydrate, 7.3 g fat, 21.1 mg sodium

BASIC SEMOLINA PASTA - NO OIL

This is for those of us watching fat intake.

	Hand	**Extruder**
durum semolina	1 cup	1⅓ cups
egg	1	1
water, if and as needed	2-3 tbs.	2-3 tbs.

per 1-cup serving   235 calories, 10.1 g protein, 42.2 g carbohydrate, 2.7 g fat, 21.1 mg sodium

BASIC SEMOLINA PASTA - NO EGG

Really keep an eye on the dough and adjust the water or flour one teaspoon at a time until the proper consistency is obtained. How basic can you get?

	Hand	Extruder
durum semolina	1 cup	1⅓ cups
water	⅓ cup	⅓ cup

per 1-cup serving   210 calories, 8.0 g protein, 42.0 g carbohydrate, 1.0 g fat, 0.8 mg sodium

SOUR CREAM PASTA

The incomplete protein in the grain is complemented by the protein in the sour cream, forming a complete protein and a more nutritious pasta.

	Hand	Extruder
durum semolina	1 cup	1¼ cups
onion powder, optional	1 tsp.	1 tsp.
sour cream	¼ cup	¼ cup
water, if and as needed	2-3 tbs.	1-2 tbs.

per 1-cup serving   251 calories, 8.6 g protein, 42.8 g carbohydrate, 5.0 g fat, 10.2 mg sodium

BUTTERMILK PASTA

The buttermilk and wheat combine nicely in this very nutritious pasta.

	Hand	Extruder
durum semolina	1 cup	1¼ cups
buttermilk	¼-⅓ cup	¼ cup
vegetable oil, optional	—	1 tsp.

per 1-cup serving   218 calories, 8.7 g protein, 43.0 g carbohydrate, 1.2 g fat, 21.4 mg sodium

MULTI-GRAIN PASTA

Use a multi-grain flour which may also be called 7, 9, or 12 grain flour — it's available in health food stores.

	Hand	Extruder
multi-grain flour	1 cup	1¼ cups
egg	1	1
vegetable oil, optional	—	1 tbs.
water, if and as needed		

per 1-cup serving   292 calories, 12.7 g protein, 53.5 g carbohydrate, 3.0 g fat, 21.0 mg sodium

100% WHOLE WHEAT PASTA

This golden brown pasta has a nice nutty flavor, good served with anything.

	Hand	Extruder
whole wheat flour	1 cup	1¼-1⅓ cups
egg	1	1
vegetable oil, optional	1 tsp.	1 tbs.
water, if and as needed	1-2 tbs.	1-2 tsp.

per 1-cup serving   158 calories, 7.4 g protein, 28.5 g carbohydrate, 2.3 g fat, 22.3 mg sodium

OAT PASTA

You can make oat flour by processing oats in a blender or food processor.

	Hand	Extruder
durum semolina	¾ cup	1 cup
oat flour	¼ cup	¼ cup
egg	1	1
vegetable oil, optional	1 tbs.	1 tbs.
water, if and as needed	1-2 tsp.	1-2 tsp.

per 1-cup serving   255 calories, 9.2 g protein, 38.1 g carbohydrate, 7.2 g fat, 21.2 mg sodium

ANCIENT GRAIN PASTA

If using an extruder, use a large die so holes don't become clogged by the grains. This is best cooked fresh as the seeds may cause the pasta to tear as it dries. The oil is always optional.

	Hand	Extruder
durum semolina	1 cup	1¼ cups
spelt flour	¼ cup	⅓ cup
quinoa grain	1 tsp.	1 tsp.
amaranth grain	1½ tsp.	1½ tsp.
egg	1	1
sunflower or vegetable oil	1 tbs.	1 tbs.
water, if and as needed	1-2 tbs.	1-2 tbs.

per 1-cup serving   364 calories, 13.4 g protein, 59.1 g carbohydrate, 8.1 g fat, 21.5 mg sodium

CORN PASTA

Use either yellow or blue cornmeal and serve with southern or southwestern meals. It could also be served as a side dish with salsa. The blue cornmeal makes a colorful, interesting pasta!

	Hand	Extruder
durum semolina	¾ cup	1 cup
cornmeal	¼ cup	¼ cup
egg	1	1
vegetable oil, optional	—	1 tbs.
water, if and as needed	2 tbs.	1 tbs.

per 1-cup serving   219 calories, 9.0 g protein, 39.3 g carbohydrate, 2.8 g fat, 52.8 mg sodium

BUCKWHEAT PASTA

This is a basic pasta with the distinctive flavoring of buckwheat. Serve with any entrée.

	Hand	**Extruder**
durum semolina	¾ cup	1 cup
buckwheat flour	¼ cup	¼ cup
vegetable oil, optional	1 tbs.	1 tbs.
egg	1	1
water, if and as needed	1-2 tbs.	1-2 tbs.

per 1-cup serving   250 calories, 9.1 g protein, 37.7 g carbohydrate, 7.2 g fat, 21.1 mg sodium

RYE PASTA

Don't roll this too thin, as the caraway seeds could cause tearing. If using an extruder, the seeds should be ground or crushed, or a large die used, so holes don't become clogged. This is great served with freshly steamed broccoli and butter, corned beef or melted American or cheddar cheese.

	Hand	Extruder
durum semolina	1 cup	1¼ cups
rye flour	¼ cup	⅓ cup
caraway seeds	1 tbs.	1⅓ tbs.
egg	1	1
vegetable oil, optional	—	1 tbs.
water, if and as needed	2-4 tbs.	2-4 tbs.

per 1-cup serving   250 calories, 9.1 g protein, 37.8 g carbohydrate, 7.1 g fat, 21.1 mg sodium

CORNELL PASTA

This is based on a formula devised by faculty at Cornell University for superior nutrition. The soy flour may be found in health food stores. It has a great nutty taste with a slightly brown color.

	Hand	**Extruder**
durum semolina	1 cup	1¼ cups
nonfat dry milk	1 tbs.	1 tbs.
soy flour	1 tbs.	1 tbs.
wheat germ	1 tbs.	1 tbs.
egg	1	1
vegetable oil, optional	1 tbs.	1 tbs.
water, if and as needed	1 tbs.	2 tbs.

per 1-cup serving   322 calories, 13.9 g protein, 47.2 g carbohydrate, 8.6 g fat, 34.7 mg sodium

THREE SEED PASTA

The sunflower seeds should be finely ground in a food processor or blender. If using an extruder, grind all seeds and use one of the large dies so holes don't become clogged. Cook and serve immediately. If using a hand machine, don't roll too thinly, as the seeds may cause tearing. I stop at the fourth level of rolling. It may be difficult to roll initially and should be run through the first set of rollers several times.

	Hand	Extruder
durum semolina	1 cup	1¼ cups
sunflower seeds, ground	1 tbs.	1 tbs.
sesame seeds	1½ tsp.	1½ tsp.
poppy seeds	1 tsp.	1 tsp.
egg	1	1
sunflower or vegetable oil, optional	1 tbs.	1 tbs.
water, if and as needed	2 tbs.	1-2 tbs.

per 1-cup serving   315 calories, 11.5 g protein, 43.5 g carbohydrate, 10.7 g fat, 58.2 mg sodium

GARBANZO OR BLACK BEAN PASTA

*Garbanzo flour may be purchased at a health food store. If you have a home mill, any bean or lentil may be milled and used in place of the garbanzo flour. A nutritious pasta which combines nicely with **Onion Dill Pasta**, page 86, or may be served alone with salsa, chili or other spicy topping.*

	Hand	Extruder
durum semolina	¾ cup	1 cup
garbanzo or black bean flour	⅓ cup	⅓ cup
onion powder, optional	⅛ tsp.	⅛ tsp.
egg	1	1
olive oil, optional	1 tsp.	1¼ tbs.
water, if and as needed	2 tbs.	1-2 tsp.

per 1-cup serving   336 calories, 13.1 g protein, 52.6 g carbohydrate, 8.4 g fat, 27.1 mg sodium

MILLET PASTA

This requires water to be added slowly, 1 tbs. at a time, and mixed well in between. Rolls and extrudes beautifully, but don't roll too thinly.

	Hand	**Extruder**
durum semolina	3/4 cup	1 cup
millet flour	1/4 cup	1/3 cup
egg	1	1
vegetable or olive oil, optional	1 tbs.	1 tbs.
water, if and as needed	1-2 tbs.	2-3 tbs.

per 1-cup serving   335 calories, 12.1 g protein, 56.2 g carbohydrate, 7.9 g fat, 21.7 mg sodium

APPLE AMARANTH PASTA

This flavorful pasta may be served with just about any sauce.

	Hand	**Extruder**
durum semolina	3/4 cup	1 cup
amaranth flour	1/4 cup	1/3 cup
apple juice	1/4-1/3 cup	1/4-1/3 cup
vegetable or olive oil, optional	1 tbs.	1 tbs.

per 1-cup serving   224 calories, 6.7 g protein, 36.8 g carbohydrate, 5.6 g fat, 0.7 mg sodium

QUINOA PASTA

Quinoa is a very high protein grain which makes this a nutritious pasta all by itself. The nutty flavor of quinoa combines nicely with vegetables or chicken. This dough may be difficult to roll in the hand machine and should not be rolled too thinly.

	Hand	Extruder
durum semolina	¾ cup	1 cup
quinoa flour	⅓ cup	⅓ cup
egg	1	1
vegetable oil, optional	—	1 tbs.
water, if and as needed	1-2 tbs.	1-2 tbs.

per 1-cup serving 238 calories, 10.6 g protein, 41.4 g carbohydrate, 3.3 g fat, 22.4 mg sodium

BARLEY PASTA

Barley imparts a slightly sweet and malty flavor. Serve with a variety of toppings.

	Hand	Extruder
durum semolina	3/4 cup	1 cup
barley flour	1/4 cup	1/4 cup
egg	1	1
vegetable oil, optional	—	1 tbs.
water, if and as needed	1-2 tbs.	1-2 tbs.

per 1-cup serving   249 calories, 10.4 g protein, 46.0 g carbohydrate, 0.5 g fat, 21.7 mg sodium

SOY PASTA

Soy flour adds a slightly nutty flavor and lots of nutrition. Serve with all sauces.

	Hand	Extruder
durum semolina	3/4 cup	1 cup
soy flour	1/4 cup	1/3 cup
soy or vegetable oil, optional	1 tbs.	1 tbs.
egg	1	1
water, if and as needed	1-2 tbs.	1-2 tbs.

per 1-cup serving   306 calories, 14.7 g protein, 37.7 g carbohydrate, 10.6 g fat, 21.3 mg sodium

AMARANTH PASTA

Another ancient grain, amaranth is very high in protein and combines nicely with tomato sauces and vegetable dishes. The walnut oil, if available, adds a nuttier taste to this already nutty pasta. Amaranth tends to get "thirsty" and seems to need more water than other grains.

	Hand	Extruder
durum semolina	¾ cup	1 cup
amaranth flour	¼ cup	⅓ cup
egg	1	1
vegetable or walnut oil, optional	1 tbs.	1 tbs.
water, if and as needed	3-4 tbs.	3-4 tbs.

per 1-cup serving 289 calories, 10.7 g protein, 43.4 g carbohydrate, 7.9 g fat, 21.3 mg sodium

RICE PASTA

Rice may be ground into flour in a regular kitchen blender or food processor provided that it has a very strong motor. Grind approximately ¼ cup at a time and be cautious about overworking the machine! Rice flour may also be purchased in some grocery stores and in health food stores. This recipe was tested using white rice flour, but brown rice may also be used.

	Hand	Extruder
durum semolina	¾ cup	1 cup
rice flour	¼ cup	¼ cup
egg	1	1
vegetable or olive oil, optional	1 tbs.	1 tbs.
water, as needed	1-2 tbs.	1-2 tbs.

per 1-cup serving   289 calories, 9.4 g protein, 46.4 g carbohydrate, 7.3 g fat, 22.7 mg sodium

TEFF PASTA

Teff is a flavorful grain which is tiny enough to use unaltered in the pasta, although teff flour works somewhat better. Teff is usually combined with spicy foods.

	Hand	Extruder
durum semolina	¾ cup	1 cup
teff flour	¼ cup	¼ cup
egg	1	1
vegetable or olive oil, optional	1 tbs.	1 tbs.
water, if and as needed		

per 1-cup serving   289 calories, 10.4 g protein, 45.4 g carbohydrate, 7.3 g fat, 24.3 mg sodium

SPICY TEFF PASTA

Teff is usually eaten with hot, spicy foods. This recipe adds some common Ethiopian spices right into the pasta.

	Hand	Extruder
durum semolina	3/4 cup	1 cup
teff flour	1/4 cup	1/4 cup
cayenne	1/4 tsp.	1/3 tsp.
black pepper	1/4 tsp.	1/4 tsp.
ground ginger	1/8 tsp.	1/8 tsp.
ground cloves	1/8 tsp.	1/8 tsp.
cinnamon	pinch	pinch
egg	1	1
vegetable or olive oil, optional	1 tbs.	1 tbs.
water, if and as needed	—	1 tbs.

per 1-cup serving   291 calories, 10.5 g protein, 45.7 g carbohydrate, 7.3 g fat, 24.7 mg sodium

AMARANTH BARLEY PASTA

Amaranth and barley combine to form a unique and very flavorful combination. Any sauce goes well with this pasta.

	Hand	Extruder
durum semolina	½ cup	⅔ cup
amaranth flour	¼ cup	⅓ cup
barley flour	¼ cup	⅓ cup
egg	1	1
walnut or vegetable oil, optional	1 tbs.	1 tbs.
water, if and as needed	1 tbs.	1 tbs.

per 1-cup serving   305 calories, 11.1 g protein, 47.2g carbohydrate, 8.2 g fat, 22.0 mg sodium

RICE MILLET PASTA

Add the water very slowly — 1/2 tablespoon at a time until the proper consistency is obtained. Serve with any sauce.

	Hand	Extruder
durum semolina	1/2 cup	2/3 cup
rice flour	1/4 cup	1/3 cup
millet flour	1/4 cup	1/3 cup
egg	1	1
walnut or vegetable oil, optional	1 tbs.	1 tbs.
water, if and as needed	1 tbs.	1 tbs.

per 1-cup serving   298 calories, 9.4 g protein, 49.9 g carbohydrate, 7.8 g fat, 23.9 mg sodium

OAT SOY PASTA

This may require several initial passes through the widest rollers, after which it rolls out nicely. It is a delicate pasta which should be dried flat or cooked immediately. A very nutritious, nutty pasta which may be served with any type of sauce.

	Hand	Extruder
durum semolina	½ cup	⅔ cup
oat flour	¼ cup	⅓ cup
soy flour	¼ cup	⅓ cup
egg	1	1
walnut or vegetable oil, optional	1 tbs.	1 tbs.
water, if and as needed	1-1 ½ tbs.	1-2 tbs.

per 1-cup serving   288 calories, 13.9 g protein, 33.6 g carbohydrate, 10.8 g fat, 21.5 mg sodium

TRITICALE PASTA

Triticale is grain which is a cross between wheat and rye and has a nutty flavor. This rolls nicely on hand machines and may be slow to extrude. Oil is optional.

	Hand	Extruder
triticale flour	1 cup	1¼ cups
egg	1	1
walnut or vegetable oil	1 tbs.	1 tbs.
water, if and as needed	1-2 tbs.	1 tbs.

per 1-cup serving   320 calories, 11.4 g protein, 54.9 g carbohydrate, 7.7 g fat, 21.0 mg sodium

TRITICALE CORN PASTA

Good tossed with grated cheddar and some caraway seeds. Oil is optional.

	Hand	Extruder
triticale flour	¾ cup	1 cup
soy flour	¼ cup	⅓ cup
egg	1	1
walnut or vegetable oil	1 tbs.	1 tbs.
water, if and as needed	2 tbs.	1 tbs.

per 1-cup serving   403 calories, 18.1g protein, 60.9 g carbohydrate, 11.3 g fat, 21.3 mg sodium

AMARANTH CORN PASTA

*Amaranth's origins are tied to the Aztecs, who combined it with corn and peppers. Serve this pasta with salsa or **Mexican Tomato Sauce**, page 147. Crushed red pepper may be substituted for the cayenne pepper if desired.*

	Hand	Extruder
durum semolina	¾ cup	1 cup
amaranth flour	¼ cup	⅓ cup
cornmeal	¼ cup	⅓ cup
cayenne	¼-½ tsp.	⅓-½ tsp.
garlic cloves, minced	1	1
egg	1	1
vegetable or walnut oil, optional	1 tbs.	1 tbs.
lime juice	2 tbs.	2 tbs.
water, if and as needed	1-2 tbs.	1-2 tbs.

per 1-cup serving   331 calories, 11.8 g protein, 52.3 g carbohydrate, 8.3 g fat, 53.6 mg sodium

CORNMEAL RYE PASTA

*This is fabulous with **Orange Beef**, page 152.*

	Hand	**Extruder**
durum semolina	3⁄4 cup	1 cup
rye flour	1⁄4 cup	1⁄3 cup
cornmeal	1⁄4 cup	1⁄3 cup
caraway seeds, optional	1 tsp.	ground - 1 tsp.
egg	1	1
vegetable or olive oil, optional	1 tbs.	1 tbs.
water, if and as needed	2-3 tbs.	2-3 tbs.

per 1-cup serving   290 calories, 10.1 g protein, 45.7 g carbohydrate, 7.5 g fat, 52.9 mg sodium

CORN RICE PASTA

A delicate pasta which should not be rolled too thinly on the hand machine. Serve in place of rice with stir-fried or Mexican meals.

	Hand	Extruder
durum semolina	½ cup	⅔ cup
rice flour	¼ cup	⅓ cup
cornmeal	¼ cup	⅓ cup
egg	1	1
walnut or vegetable oil, optional	1 tbs.	1 tbs.
water, if and as needed	¼ cup	1 tbs.

per 1-cup serving   276 calories, 8.4 g protein, 44.1 g carbohydrate, 7.4 g fat, 54.9 mg sodium

HERBS AND SPICES

   If serving one of these pastas as a side dish with only butter or olive oil, you may increase the amount of herbs and/or spices for a stronger flavor. The flavor of the pasta should not overwhelm a topping or sauce but should complement it nicely.

   When choosing a pasta made with herbs and spices, look at the meal in which you plan to serve it and consider what herbs or spices are used. You may wish to select a pasta which has some or all of the same herbs and/or spices.

   My objective in developing these recipes was to create pastas which blend easily with just about any meal, as well as pastas which are very specialized and different, such as the curry and graham masala. These pastas are unique alternatives to rice.

SPICY SOUTHWESTERN PASTA

*The cayenne may be adjusted to your taste. Serve this pasta with **Mexican Tomato Sauce**, page 147, **Indonesian Peanut Sauce**, page 148, or simply toss with salsa for a quick and easy throw-together.*

	Hand	Extruder
durum semolina	1 cup	1¼ cups
cilantro, dried, optional	1 tsp.	1 tsp.
OR fresh cilantro, chopped, optional	1 tbs.	—
cayenne or chile powder	¼ tsp.	⅓ tsp.
onion powder	¼ tsp.	⅓ tsp.
egg	1	1
olive oil, optional	1 tbs.	1 tbs.
water, if and as needed	1-2 tbs.	1-2 tbs.

per 1-cup serving   276 calories, 10.1 g protein, 42.4 g carbohydrate, 7.4 g fat, 21.3 mg sodium

SPICY HERB PASTA

Some people always prefer fresh herbs if using the hand machines; triple the amount given. Goes well with anything.

	Hand	**Extruder**
durum semolina	1 cup	1¼ cups
oregano	¼ tsp.	¼ tsp.
thyme	⅛ tsp.	⅛ tsp.
black pepper	¼ tsp.	¼ tsp.
parsley, dried	⅓ tsp.	⅓ tsp.
celery seed	pinch	pinch
egg	1	1
vegetable oil, optional	1 tbs.	1 tbs.
water, if and as needed	2-4 tbs.	2-4 tbs.

per 1-cup serving   277 calories, 10.2 g protein, 42.5 g carbohydrate, 7.2 g fat, 22.0 mg sodium

PARSLEY HERB PASTA

Fresh herbs may be substituted if using the hand machines; simply triple the amount given. Serve as a side dish with grilled steak or chicken or serve with any seafood or poultry and sauce using parsley, celery seed or tarragon.

	Hand	Extruder
durum semolina	1 cup	1¼ cups
chives	⅛ tsp.	⅛ tsp.
tarragon	¼ tsp.	¼ tsp.
parsley, dried	1 tsp.	1⅓ tsp.
celery seed	pinch	pinch
egg	1	1
vegetable oil, optional	1 tbs.	1 tbs.
water, if and as needed	2-4 tbs.	2-4 tbs.

per 1-cup serving   277 calories, 10.2 g protein, 42.5 g carbohydrate, 7.2 g fat, 23.3 mg sodium

JALAPEÑO PASTA

*Toss with salsa as a side dish or serve with **Mexican Tomato Sauce**, page 147. Jalapeño flakes may be found in well stocked spice sections of grocery stores or in gourmet shops. If using canned jalapeños, use the liquid in which they are packed for extra jalapeño flavoring!*

	Hand	**Extruder**
durum semolina	1 cup	1¼ cups
jalapeño flakes, dried	½-1 tsp.	½-1 tsp.
OR diced jalapeño	1-2	1-2
egg	1	1
vegetable oil, optional	—	1 tbs.
water, if and as needed	1-2 tbs.	1-2 tbs.
(or jalapeño liquid)		

per 1-cup serving   237 calories, 10.2 g protein, 42.7 g carbohydrate, 2.7 g fat, 47.2 mg sodium

PEPPER CHIVE PASTA

The pepper should be coarse and freshly ground. Serve as a side dish with grilled steak or chicken. This pasta is excellent with any seafood or poultry sauce that contains parsley and/or onions.

	Hand	Extruder
durum semolina	1 cup	1¼ cups
chives, dried	½ tsp.	½ tsp.
black pepper	1 tsp.	1⅓ tsp.
eggs	1	1
vegetable oil, optional	1 tbs.	1 tbs.
water, if and as needed	2-4 tbs.	1-2 tbs.

per 1-cup serving   277 calories, 10.1 g protein, 42.7 g carbohydrate, 7.2 g fat, 21.4 mg sodium

MINT PASTA

If using fresh mint with a hand machine, triple the amount. Serve with lamb, or a Greek- or Middle Eastern-flavored meal. Use lemon pepper or peel if you want a spicier or sweeter pasta.

	Hand	Extruder
durum semolina	1 cup	1⅓ cups
mint, dried	1 tsp.	1¼ tsp.
lemon pepper or peel	½ tsp.	½ tsp.
egg	1	1
olive oil, optional	—	1 tbs.
water, if and as needed	1-2 tbs.	1-2 tsp.

per 1-cup serving   276 calories, 10.2 g protein, 42.5 g carbohydrate, 7.3 g fat, 21.9 mg sodium

ANISE PASTA

Anise seeds may be used whole in a hand machine or in an extruder as long as the pasta die is not too small, which could cause blockage. If desired, measure and grind the seeds with a mortar and pestle first. This makes an interesting and flavorful side dish with butter and freshly grated Parmesan cheese, or toss the pasta with freshly steamed vegetables and butter.

	Hand	**Extruder**
durum semolina	1 cup	1⅓ cups
anise seeds	1½-2 tsp.	1½-2 tsp.
egg	1	1
olive oil, optional	1 tsp.	1 tbs.
water, if and as needed	1-2 tbs.	1-2 tbs.

per 1-cup serving   252 calories, 10.3 g protein, 42.8 g carbohydrate, 0.7 g fat, 21.0 mg sodium

FENNEL PASTA

Serve with a basic tomato sauce and Italian sausage. Fennel seeds may be used whole in a hand machine or in an extruder as long as the pasta die is not too small, which could cause tearing. If desired, measure and grind the seeds with a mortar and pestle first.

	Hand	**Extruder**
durum semolina	1 cup	1⅓ cups
fennel seeds	1½-2 tsp.	1½-2 tsp.
egg	1	1
olive oil, optional	1 tsp.	1 tbs.
water, if and as needed	1-2 tbs.	1-2 tbs.

---

per 1-cup serving   252 calories, 10.2 g protein, 42.8 g carbohydrate, 4.4 g fat, 22.0 mg sodium

POPPY SEED PASTA

Serve with a lemon chicken or a lemon sauce. This is better served fresh or dried flat, as the seeds may cause the pasta to break if hung to dry.

	Hand	**Extruder**
durum semolina	1 cup	1⅓ cups
lemon peel, grated	1 tsp.	1¼ tsp.
poppy seeds	2 tsp.	2 tsp.
egg	1	1
vegetable oil, optional	—	1 tbs.
water, if and as needed	1-2 tbs.	1-2 tbs.

per 1-cup serving   245 calories, 10.4 g protein, 42.5 g carbohydrate, 3.5 g fat, 21.7 mg sodium

CHERVIL PASTA

Serve with poultry, seafood or a tomato sauce.

	Hand	**Extruder**
durum semolina	1 cup	1⅓ cups
chervil	1 tsp.	1 tsp.
sour cream or nonfat plain yogurt	¼-⅓ cup	⅓ cup
vegetable oil, optional	—	1 tbs.

per 1-cup serving   251 calories, 8.6 g protein, 42.8 g carbohydrate, 5.0 g fat, 10.2 mg sodium

SESAME PASTA

Serve this pasta in place of rice with a stir-fry. Make the thinnest noodle possible with your machine, parboil (boil until just tender) and remove. Stir-fry the noodles until crisp, or serve your stir-fry over cooked noodles. Sesame oil is not optional.

	Hand	**Extruder**
durum semolina	1 cup	1¼ cups
sesame oil	1 tbs.	1⅓ tbs.
water, as needed	¼-⅓ cup	¼-⅓ cup

per 1-cup serving   250 calories, 8.0 g protein, 42.0 g carbohydrate, 5.5 g fat, 0.6 mg sodium

HERB PASTA

For a flavorful side dish, toss pasta with a small amount of melted butter or olive oil, Italian seasoning and some freshly grated Parmesan cheese. Italian seasoning blends may be found in the spice section of your grocery store and may be adjusted to taste if desired.

	Hand	Extruder
durum semolina	1 cup	1⅓ cups
Italian seasonings, dried	1 tsp.	1 tsp.
vegetable or olive oil, optional	—	1 tbs.
water	¼–⅓ cup	¼ cup

per 1-cup serving   210 calories, 8.0 g protein, 42.0 g carbohydrate, 1.0 g fat, 0.6 mg sodium

MEXICAN HERB PASTA

The amount of cilantro may be adjusted to your taste. Serve with salsa or a basic cream sauce and cilantro. Dried cilantro works better in the electric extruders, but either may be used with the hand-crank machines.

	Hand	**Extruder**
durum semolina	1 cup	1¼ cups
cilantro, dried	1 tsp.	1 tsp.
OR fresh cilantro, chopped	1 tbs.	1 tbs.
olive or vegetable oil, optional	1 tbs.	1 tbs.
water, as needed	¼-⅓ cup	¼-⅓ cup

per 1-cup serving   250 calories, 8.0 g protein, 42.0 g carbohydrate, 5.7 g fat, 0.6 mg sodium

LEMON OREGANO PASTA

Lemon pasta is great with a Greek-style dinner or with fish or chicken.

	Hand	**Extruder**
durum semolina	1 cup	1½ cups
oregano, dried or liquid	1 tsp.	1 tsp.
OR fresh oregano, chopped	1 tbs.	—
vegetable oil, optional	—	1 tbs.
egg	1	1
lemon juice	2 tbs.	1½-2 tbs.
water, if and as needed		1 tbs.

VARIATIONS

- **Lemon Pepper:** Omit the oregano and use 1 tsp. of coarsely ground black pepper.

- **Lemon Dill:** Omit the oregano and use 1 tsp. dill weed.

- **Lemon Rosemary:** Omit the oregano and use 1 tsp. rosemary leaves.

per 1-cup serving   239 calories, 10.2 g protein, 43.2 g carbohydrate, 2.8 g fat, 23.2 mg sodium

YOGURT LEMON PEPPER PASTA

This rolls out beautifully and is out of this world. Serve with poultry, seafood or a lemon cream sauce.

	Hand	Extruder
durum semolina	1 cup	1¼ cups
oregano, dried	½ tsp.	½ tsp.
OR fresh oregano, chopped	1½ tsp.	—
coarsely ground black pepper	½ tsp.	½ tsp.
plain nonfat yogurt	¼ cup	3 tbs.
olive or vegetable oil, optional	—	1 tbs.
lemon juice	1 tbs.	1 tbs.
water, if and as needed		

per 1-cup serving   222 calories, 9.0 g protein, 43.3 g carbohydrate, 1.3 g fat, 13.3 mg sodium

LEMON CHIVE PASTA

This flavorful pasta nicely complements seafood or poultry that has been cooked with lemon and onions.

	Hand	Extruder
durum semolina	1 cup	1⅓ cups
lemon pepper	½-1 tsp.	½-1 tsp.
chives, dried	2 tsp.	2 tsp.
lemon juice	2 tbs.	2 tbs.
vegetable or olive oil, optional	—	1½ tsp.
water, as needed	¼ cup	¼-⅓ cup

per 1-cup serving   212 calories, 8.0 g protein, 42.7 g carbohydrate, 1.0 g fat, 2.7 mg sodium

GINGER PASTA

Serve with or in place of rice with any stir-fry or Oriental-style meal.

	Hand	Extruder
durum semolina	1 cup	1¼ cups
egg	1	1
ground ginger	½ tsp.	½ tsp.
garlic clove, minced	1	1
water, if and as needed	1-2 tbs.	1-2 tbs.

per 1-cup serving   237 calories, 10.2 g protein, 42.8 g carbohydrate, 2.7 g fat, 21.5 mg sodium

CURRY PASTA

A savory complement to poultry, seafood or vegetables.

	Hand	Extruder
durum semolina	1 cup	1⅓ cups
curry powder	1 tsp.	1¼ tsp.
egg	1	1
vegetable oil, optional	—	1 tbs.
water, if and as needed	1-2 tbs.	1-2 tbs.

per 1-cup serving   237 calories, 10.2 g protein, 42.6 g carbohydrate, 2.8 g fat, 21.3 mg sodium

AFGHANISTAN CURRY PASTA

Serve this in place of rice with your favorite curry.

	Hand	**Extruder**
durum semolina	1 cup	1⅓ cups
curry powder	1 tsp.	1¼ tsp.
cinnamon	½ tsp.	½ tsp.
ground cloves	½ tsp.	½ tsp.
ground cardamom	½ tsp.	½ tsp.
egg	1	1
vegetable oil, optional	—	1 tbs.
water, if and as needed	1-2 tbs.	1-2 tbs.

per 1-cup serving   240 calories, 10.2 g protein, 43.4 g carbohydrate, 2.9 g fat, 22.3 mg sodium

WEST INDIAN CURRY PASTA

This bright yellow pasta has lots of flavor! Serve with curried chicken.

	Hand	Extruder
durum semolina	1 cup	1⅓ cups
curry powder	1 tsp.	1¼ tsp.
ground coriander	⅓ tsp.	⅓ tsp.
anise seeds	½ tsp.	½ tsp.
black pepper	⅓ tsp.	⅓ tsp.
cinnamon	⅓ tsp.	⅓ tsp.
ground ginger	⅓ tsp.	⅓ tsp.
ground turmeric	⅓ tsp.	⅓ tsp.
egg	1	1
vegetable oil, optional	—	1 tbs.
water, if and as needed	1-2 tbs.	1-2 tbs.

per 1-cup serving   266 calories, 12.4 g protein, 43.6 g carbohydrate, 4.5 g fat, 42.8 mg sodium

RED PEPPER PASTA

*Perk up any meal with this hot and spicy pasta. The spicing is to my taste, and you may adjust if desired. Serve with salsa, a spicy chicken or seafood topping or with **Mexican Tomato Sauce**, page 147.*

	Hand	Extruder
durum semolina	1 cup	1⅓ cups
crushed red pepper	1½ tsp.	1¾ tsp.
1 egg	1	1
vegetable oil, optional	—	1 tbs.
water, if and as needed	1-2 tbs.	1-2 tbs.

per 1-cup serving   238 calories, 10.2 g protein, 42.9 g carbohydrate, 2.7 g fat, 21.5 mg sodium

THREE PEPPER PASTA

A very hot pasta — serve it with salsa, any spicy entrée, or chile. Seasoning may be adjusted to your taste.

	Hand	**Extruder**
durum semolina	1 cup	1⅓ cups
coarsely ground black pepper	½ tsp.	½ tsp.
crushed red pepper	½ tsp.	½ tsp.
ground white pepper	½ tsp.	½ tsp.
plain nonfat yogurt	¼ cup	¼ cup
vegetable oil, optional	—	1 tbs.
water, if and as needed		

per 1-cup serving   222 calories, 9.0 g protein, 43.3 g carbohydrate, 1.3 g fat, 13.3 mg sodium

SOUTHWESTERN CORN PASTA

If using fresh cilantro with the hand-cranked machine, triple the amount given. This complements any and all Mexican or hot and spicy meals.

	Hand	**Extruder**
durum semolina	¾ cup	1 cup
cornmeal	¼ cup	⅓ cup
egg	1	1
cilantro, dried	1-1½ tsp.	1-1½ tbs.
crushed red pepper	½ tsp.	⅔ tsp.
vegetable or olive oil, optional	—	1 tbs.
water, if and as needed	2 tbs.	2 tbs.

per 1-cup serving   272 calories, 11.0 g protein, 49.8 g carbohydrate, 3.0 g fat, 52.2 mg sodium

CAJUN PASTA

Cajun spice mixes are made by Paul Prudhome or McCormick Shilling and are usually found in the spice section of your grocery store. I use the Cajun chicken spices and serve this pasta topped with **Cajun Shrimp**, page 138, or any spicy entrée.

	Hand	Extruder
durum semolina	1 cup	1¼ cups
egg	1	1
Cajun spices	1-1½ tsp.	1-1½ tsp.
vegetable oil, optional	—	1 tbs.
water, if and as needed	1-2 tbs.	1 tbs.

per 1-cup serving   235 calories, 10.1 g protein, 42.2 g carbohydrate, 2.7 gg fat, 21.0 mg sodium

SAFFRON PASTA

If using saffron threads, warm the water (microwave for 1 minute) and soak the threads in the water. Serve with poultry or seafood.

	Hand	**Extruder**
durum semolina	1 cup	1 cup
ground saffron or threads	1/8-1/4 tsp.	1/8-1/4 tsp.
vegetable oil, optional	—	1 tbs.
water, as needed	1/3 cup	1/4 cup

per 1-cup serving   210 calories, 8.1 g protein, 42.0 g carbohydrate, 1.0 g fat, 0.8 mg sodium

DILLY PASTA

Serve as a side dish with chicken or as ravoli dough with a cheese filling.

	Hand	**Extruder**
durum semolina	1 cup	1 1/4 cups
dill weed	1 1/2 tsp.	1 3/4 tsp.
egg	1	1
vegetable oil, optional	—	1 tbs.
water, if and as needed	2 tbs.	1-2 tbs.

per 1-cup serving   237 calories, 10.2 g protein, 42.5 g carbohydrate, 2.7 g fat, 22.2 mg sodium

NUTMEG PASTA

Freshly grated nutmeg, if available, is superior in this flavorful pasta. Serve with butter and Parmesan cheese or tomato sauce as a side dish, or serve with any meal which uses nutmeg as an ingredient to complement and enhance the flavor.

	Hand	Extruder
durum semolina	1 cup	1¼ cups
ground nutmeg	1 tsp.	1 tsp.
egg	1	1
vegetable oil, optional	1 tsp.	1 tbs.
water, if and as needed	2 tbs.	2 tbs.

per 1-cup serving   252 calories, 10.1 g protein, 42.6 g carbohydrate, 4.4 g fat, 21.1 mg sodium

SOUR CREAM CHIVE PASTA

What a wonderful side dish to serve with a grilled steak! Very colorful and flavorful. This recipe seemed very temperamental in the extruders and is therefore rated "Advanced" for extruders. Add the sour cream to the semolina and let the machine knead longer than usual.

	Hand	**Extruder**
durum semolina	1 cup	1¼ cups
chives, dried	½-1 tsp.	½-1 tsp.
sour cream	¼ cup	¼ cup
water, if and as needed	1-2 tbs.	1-2 tbs.

per 1-cup serving   251 calories, 8.6 g protein, 42.8 g carbohydrate, 5.0 g fat, 10.2 mg sodium

LIME CILANTRO PASTA

Serve this tossed with a flavorful salsa, black beans, chicken or any Mexican meal. Water may not be needed and should be added very slowly if used.

	Hand	Extruder
durum semolina	1 cup	1¼ cups
cilantro, dried	1 tsp.	1¼ tsp.
OR fresh cilantro, chopped	1 tbs.	—
vegetable oil, optional	—	1 tbs.
egg	1	1
lime juice	2 tbs.	2 tbs.
water, if needed		

per 1-cup serving 235 calories, 10.1 g protein, 42.2 g carbohydrate, 2.7 g fat, 21.0 mg sodium

OLD BAY PASTA

Use your favorite seafood seasoning in this delicious pasta to serve with any fresh, steamed seafood (I serve with shrimp). The seasoning amount may be adjusted to taste. Add water slowly.

	Hand	**Extruder**
durum semolina	1 cup	1⅓ cups
Old Bay™ seasoning	1-1½ tsp.	1-1¾ tsp.
egg	1	1
vegetable oil, optional	—	1 tbs.
water, if and as needed	1-2 tbs.	1-2 tbs.

per 1-cup serving   235 calories, 10.1 g protein, 42.2 g carbohydrate, 2.7 g fat, 21.0 mg sodium

SCARBOROUGH "FARE" PASTA

You can't make this without humming the song. A great, flavorful pasta with just butter and Parmesan cheese or serve with **Scarborough Tomato Sauce***, page 146, poultry or seafood.*

	Hand	Extruder
durum semolina	1 cup	1⅓ cups
parsley, dried	½-1 tsp.	½-1 tsp.
sage, dried	¼ tsp.	¼ tsp.
rosemary, dried	¼ tsp.	¼ tsp.
thyme	¼ tsp.	¼ tsp.
egg	1	1
vegetable or olive oil, optional	1 tbs.	1 tbs.
water, if and as needed	1 tbs.	2 tbs.

per 1-cup serving 276 calories, 10.2 g protein, 42.5 g carbohydrate, 7.2 g fat, 22.2 mg sodium

FIVE-SPICE PASTA

*Serve this in place of rice, tossed or topped with your favorite Chinese stir-fry, or **Indonesian Peanut Sauce**, page 148. Five-spice powder blends are available in gourmet or large grocery stores either in the spice or Oriental food section, or in Chinese groceries.*

	Hand	Extruder
durum semolina	1 cup	1⅓ cups
five-spice powder blend	1 tsp.	1 tsp.
egg	1	1
vegetable oil, optional	—	1 tbs.
water, if and as needed	1-2 tbs.	1-2 tbs.

per 1-cup serving 235 calories, 10.1 g protein, 42.2 g carbohydrate, 2.7 g fat, 21.0 mg sodium

MUSTARD PASTA

*This is great with **Scarborough Tomato Sauce**, page 146, or any other tomato sauce, or as a side dish with ham.*

	Hand	Extruder
durum semolina	1 cup	1¼ cups
dry mustard	½ tsp.	½ tsp.
rosemary leaves, dried	pinch	pinch
onion powder	¼ tsp.	¼ tsp.
garlic cloves, minced	1-2	1-2
egg	1	1
vegetable oil, optional	1 tsp.	1 tsp.
water, if and as needed	—	

per 1-cup serving   253 calories, 10.3 g protein, 42.9 g carbohydrate, 4.3 g fat, 21.4 mg sodium

FLAVORFUL HERBED PASTA

*Serve this colorful pasta with **Scarborough Tomato Sauce**, page 146, or tossed with butter and freshly grated Parmesan cheese. A great side dish for a grilled steak!*

	Hand	Extruder
durum semolina	1 cup	1⅓ cups
thyme, dried	¼ tsp.	¼ tsp.
sage, dried	¼ tsp.	¼ tsp.
paprika	¼ tsp.	¼ tsp.
egg	1	1
vegetable oil, optional	—	1 tbs.
water, if and as needed	2 tbs.	1-2 tbs.

per 1-cup serving   236 calories, 10.1 g protein, 42.4 g carbohydrate, 2.7 g fat, 21.1 mg sodium

GINGERBREAD PASTA

This flavorful, dark colored pasta is great during the holiday season. Simply serve with butter and freshly grated cheese as a side dish.

	Hand	Extruder
durum semolina	1 cup	1¼ cups
ground ginger	½ tsp.	½ tsp.
cinnamon	¼ tsp.	¼ tsp.
nutmeg	dash	dash
ground cloves	dash	dash
dried orange peel, optional	⅛ tsp.	⅛ tsp.
egg	1	1
vegetable oil, optional	1 tbs.	1 tbs.
water, if and as needed	0-1 tbs.	1 tbs.

per 1-cup serving   277 calories, 10.1 g protein, 42.7 g carbohydrate, 7.2 g fat, 21.3 mg sodium

GARLIC OREGANO PASTA

Liquid garlic juice may be used in place of minced or pressed garlic. This pasta is wonderful with your favorite tomato sauce or as a side dish to any meat. Both the garlic and oregano may be adjusted to your taste.

	Hand	Extruder
durum semolina	1 cup	1¼ cups
oregano, dried	1 tbs.	1 tbs.
OR fresh oregano, chopped	3 tbs.	—
egg	1	1
garlic cloves, minced	1	1
olive oil, optional	1 tbs.	1 tbs.
water, if and as needed		

---

per 1-cup serving 281 calories, 10.3 g protein, 43.5 g carbohydrate, 7.5 g fat, 21.5 mg sodium

ONION DILL PASTA

Serve with your favorite herbed (such as with dill) fish or chicken. This may require several passes through the initial width of hand rollers after which it rolls nicely.

	Hand	Extruder
durum semolina	1 cup	1¼ cups
onion powder	½ tsp.	½ tsp.
dill weed	1 tsp.	1 tsp.
dry mustard	pinch	dash
egg	1	1
vegetable or olive oil, optional	—	1 tbs.
water, if and as needed	1 tbs.	

per 1-cup serving   237 calories, 10.2 g protein, 42.7 g carbohydrate, 2.7 g fat, 21.9 mg sodium

ALLSPICE PASTA

*Serve this with Swedish meatballs, any tomato sauce or with **Orange Cranberry Chicken**, page 142. It combines nicely with **Beet** and/or **Carrot Pasta**, pages 101 and 100.*

	Hand	Extruder
durum semolina	1 cup	1⅓ cups
allspice	1 tsp.	1 tsp.
egg	1	1
vegetable or olive oil, optional	1 tbs.	1 tbs.
water, if and as needed	1-2 tbs.	1-2 tbs.

per 1-cup serving   277 calories, 10.1 g protein, 42.7 g carbohydrate, 7.3 g fat, 21.5 mg sodium

ROSEMARY PEPPER PASTA

Liquid garlic juice may be used in place of minced or pressed garlic cloves, and I often prefer it, especially if extruding. The rosemary may be adjusted to your taste. This goes well with lamb, poultry, seafood, tomato or fruit sauces.

	Hand	Extruder
durum semolina	1 cup	1⅓ cups
black pepper	¼ tsp.	¼ tsp.
rosemary, dried	¼-½ tsp.	¼-½ tsp.
garlic cloves, minced	1-2	1-2
egg	1	1
olive oil, optional	1 tbs.	1 tbs.
water, if and as needed	1 tbs.	2 tbs.

per 1-cup serving   277 calories, 10.2 g protein, 42.7 g carbohydrate, 7.4 g fat, 21.5 mg sodium

PEPPER CORN PASTA

Use either yellow or blue cornmeal and serve with southern or southwestern meals. It could also be served with salsa as a side dish. The blue cornmeal makes a colorful, interesting pasta! The red pepper and onion powder give extra flavor.

	Hand	Extruder
durum semolina	¾ cup	1 cup
cornmeal	¼ cup	¼ cup
black pepper, coarsely ground	¼ tsp.	⅓ tsp.
crushed red pepper	⅓ tsp.	½ tsp.
oregano, dried	⅓ tsp.	⅓ tsp.
OR fresh oregano, chopped	1 tsp.	—
garlic cloves, minced	1	1
egg	1	1
vegetable oil, optional	—	1 tbs.
water	2 tbs.	2 tbs.

per 1-cup serving   222 calories, 9.1 g protein, 40.0 g carbohydrate, 2.8 g fat, 53.4 mg sodium

INDIAN MASALA PASTA

Masala is a blend of various spices used in Indian cooking. I have taken one of the many blends and put it right into the pasta. Serve this pungent pasta with meat or poultry which is cooked with lots of onions and garlic!

	Hand	Extruder
durum semolina	1 cup	1¼ cups
cinnamon	½ tsp.	½ tsp.
ground cumin	⅓ tsp.	⅓ tsp.
ground coriander	¼ tsp.	¼ tsp.
ground cardamom	⅛ tsp.	⅛ tsp.
black pepper, coarsely ground	⅛ tsp.	⅛ tsp.
ground cloves	pinch	pinch
mace	pinch	pinch
egg	1	1
vegetable oil, optional	—	1 tbs.
water, if and as needed	2-3 tbs.	1-2 tbs.

per 1-cup serving 238 calories, 10.2 g protein, 42.8 g carbohydrate, 2.8 g fat, 21.8 mg sodium

CINNAMON PASTA

This is delicious served with **Greek Spaghetti Sauce**, *page 145, or chicken. Cinnamon is often used in Greek and Mexican cooking.*

	Hand	**Extruder**
durum semolina	1 cup	1⅓ cups
cinnamon	½-1 tsp.	½-1 tsp.
garlic clove, minced	1-2	1-2
egg	1	1
vegetable or olive oil, optional	1 tbs.	1 tbs.
water, if and as needed	1 tbs.	2 tbs.

per 1-cup serving   277 calories, 10.2 g protein, 42.8 g carbohydrate, 7.2 g fat, 21.4 mg sodium

FOUR-SPICE PASTA

This is a typical European spice blend. This pasta goes nicely with just about anything, including all tomato or cheese sauces.

	Hand	**Extruder**
durum semolina	1 cup	1¼ cups
black pepper, coarsely ground	¼-½ tsp.	⅓-½ tsp.
ground nutmeg	⅛-¼ tsp.	⅛-¼ tsp.
ground cloves	⅛ tsp.	⅛ tsp.
ground ginger	⅛ tsp.	⅛ tsp.
egg	1	1
vegetable oil, optional	1 tbs.	1 tbs.
water, if and as needed	1-2 tbs.	1-2 tbs.

per 1-cup serving   276 calories, 10.1 g protein, 42.5 g carbohydrate, 7.3 g fat, 21.3 mg sodium

BAHARAT PASTA

Baharat is a hot blend of spices used in Middle Eastern cooking. This pasta goes nicely with a stir-fry or a basic cheese sauce with or without extra seasonings.

	Hand	Extruder
durum semolina	1 cup	1¼ cups
chili powder	pinch	pinch
cinnamon	⅛ tsp.	⅛ tsp.
ground cardamom	⅛ tsp.	⅛ tsp.
ground nutmeg	¼ tsp.	¼ tsp.
ground cloves	¼ tsp.	¼ tsp.
black pepper	¼ tsp.	¼ tsp.
coriander	¼ tsp.	¼ tsp.
cumin	¼ tsp.	¼ tsp.
paprika	½ tsp.	½ tsp.
egg	1	1
vegetable oil, optional	1 tbs.	1 tbs.
water, if and as needed	2-3 tbs.	2-3 tbs.

per 1-cup serving   279 calories, 10.2 g protein, 43.0 g carbohydrate, 7.4 g fat, 22.6 mg sodium

PARSLEY PEPPER PASTA

A wonderful pasta, this may be served with any food ranging from Italian to Greek to Mexican.

	Hand	Extruder
durum semolina	1 cup	1¼ cups
black pepper, coarsely ground	½-1 tsp.	½-1 tsp.
parsley, dried	1-2 tsp.	1-2 tsp.
OR fresh parsley, chopped	1-2 tbs.	—
egg	1	1
vegetable or olive oil, optional	1 tbs.	1 tbs.
water, if and as needed	1-2 tbs.	1-2 tbs.

per 1-cup serving   277 calories, 10.2 g protein, 42.7 g carbohydrate, 7.2 g fat, 23.1 mg sodium

BASIL OREGANO PASTA

Serve this flavorful pasta with any tomato sauce, pesto or a cream sauce flavored with basil and/or oregano.

	Hand	Extruder
durum semolina	1 cup	1¼ cups
basil, dried	1 tsp.	1 tsp.
OR fresh basil, chopped	1 tbs.	—
oregano, dried	1 tsp.	1 tsp.
OR fresh oregano, chopped	1 tbs.	—
black pepper, optional	½-1 tsp.	½-1 tsp.
egg	1	1
vegetable oil, optional	1 tbs.	1 tbs.
water, if and as needed	1-2 tbs.	1-2 tbs.

per 1-cup serving   278 calories, 10.2 g protein, 43.1 g carbohydrate, 7.3 g fat, 21.4 mg sodium

VEGETABLES AND FRUITS

TOMATO CHIVE PASTA

An interesting twist to an old favorite which may be served with any tomato sauce. The chives may be adjusted to your taste. Liquid garlic juice may be used instead of minced or pressed garlic.

	Hand	**Extruder**
durum semolina	1 cup	1¼ cups
chives, dried	1½ tsp.	1½ tsp.
garlic cloves, minced	1-2	1-2
vegetable or olive oil, optional	—	1 tbs.
tomato juice	¼-⅓ cup	¼-⅓ cup

per 1-cup serving   217 calories, 8.3 g protein, 43.5 g carbohydrate, 1.0 g fat, 41.2 mg sodium

TOMATO BASIL PASTA

This is a superb pasta with any tomato-based sauce. For real eye appeal, try combining this with spinach pasta. The basil may be adjusted to your taste.

	Hand	**Extruder**
durum semolina	1 cup	1¼ cups
basil, dried	1 tsp.	1 tsp.
OR fresh basil, chopped	1 tbs.	—
vegetable or olive oil, optional	—	1 tbs.
tomato juice	¼-⅓ cup	¼-⅓ cup

per 1-cup serving   162 calories, 6.3 g protein, 32.7 g carbohydrate, 0.8 g fat, 40.7 mg sodium

ARTICHOKE PASTA

The artichoke hearts should be marinated in oil as purchased in the grocery store. For ease of pasta making, they should be pureed in a food processor or blender. No additional oil is required in the extruder recipe, as it is already in the marinade. If using fresh parsley with the hand extruder, triple the amount. If you elect to drain the artichokes, some water may need to be added. Cook this fresh and do not allow to dry.

	Hand	**Extruder**
durum semolina	1 cup	1¼ cups
parsley, dried, optional	1½ tsp.	2 tsp.
artichoke hearts, marinated	¼–⅓ cup	¼ cup
lemon juice	1 tsp.	1¼ tsp.

per 1-cup serving   164 calories, 6.3 g protein, 33.1 g carbohydrate, 0.8 g fat, 9.5 mg sodium

CARROT PASTA

The cooked and pureed carrots provide a brilliant orange color to this pasta, as well as providing extra flavor and nutrition. The moisture comes from the carrots themselves, so allow the dough to knead prior to adding any additional water. If you are not in the mood to cook and puree carrots, simply use a jar of baby food carrots. As moisture content of fruits and vegetables varies, add more carrot puree, water or flour as necessary. Watch the dough carefully and adjust flour or water as necessary.

	Hand	**Extruder**
durum semolina	1 cup	1¼ cups
nutmeg	⅛ tsp.	⅛ tsp.
carrot puree	⅓ cup	3-5 tbs.
vegetable oil, optional	—	1 tbs.
water, if and as needed		

VARIATIONS

● Substitute ground coriander or cardamom for the nutmeg.

per 1-cup serving   215 calories, 8.1 g protein, 43.2 g carbohydrate, 1.0 g fat, 4.2 mg sodium

BEET PASTA

A flavorful and colorful pasta which is great when combined with carrot, spinach and tomato pastas. Fresh, cooked beets or rinsed, canned beets may be pureed in a food processor or blender (or just use baby food!). The moisture content of the beets may throw off the balance in the dough. Knead the dough sufficiently to pull all moisture out of the beets before adding water. Add water or semolina as necessary.

	Hand	**Extruder**
durum semolina	1 cup	1¼ cups
dill weed, optional	½ tsp.	½ tsp.
AND/OR chervil, optional	⅓ tsp.	⅓ tsp.
beet puree	⅓ cup	¼ cup
vegetable oil, optional	—	1 tbs.
water, if and as needed	2 tbs.	2 tbs.

per 1-cup serving   217 calories, 8.2 g protein, 43.3 g carbohydrate, 1.0 g fat, 9.3 mg sodium

SPINACH PASTA

Cook and drain the chopped spinach, reserving the liquid in case more moisture is required for the dough. This may be difficult to roll out the first time through a hand-crank machine. Simply repeat the process using the rollers at the widest point until it rolls through smoothly. Don't be too quick to add water to the dough in the extruder as moisture is obtained from the spinach itself during both the kneading and extruding. If dough becomes too sticky in the extruder, add a little more flour to mix if your machine allows, or dust with flour as it extrudes to prevent sticking. This recipe may be difficult to work at first, but results in a flavorful tasting spinach pasta. Notice that this recipe makes twice the usual amount.

	Hand	**Extruder**
durum semolina	2 cups	2¾ cups
chopped spinach, cooked	1 pkg. (10 oz.)	1 pkg. (10 oz.)

VARIATION

- If using with a Greek-type sauce, add ½-1 tsp. of grated lemon peel.

per 1-cup serving   219 calories, 9.1 g protein, 43.4 g carbohydrate, 1.1 g fat, 27.2 mg sodium

ZUCCHINI PASTA

The zucchini may be diced or grated; I use a food processor. The zucchini provides moisture to the dough, which may require a longer kneading than usual. As the moisture content of the zucchini itself varies, watch the dough carefully for texture. If water is added too soon, by the time the zucchini kneads in properly, the dough may become too sticky. If so, simply add more flour until the proper consistency is obtained. This recipe is not recommended for extruder machines. Toss with freshly steamed vegetables, a little butter and some fresh herbs. A gardener's delight!

Hand Only

durum semolina	1 cup
zucchini, finely diced	½ cup
water only if needed	

per 1-cup serving   213 calories, 8.3 g protein, 42.6 g carbohydrate, 1.0 g fat, 0.7 mg sodium

BROCCOLI PASTA

This dough requires extra kneading as the moisture is derived from the broccoli itself. If the dough becomes too sticky, simply add more semolina as necessary. Water may be added, but only after the dough has been kneaded to sufficiently draw out the liquids. Adjust the consistency of the dough with water or flour as needed. This recipe is not recommended for extruder machines. Toss with grated cheddar cheese or melted American cheese and caraway seeds or with freshly steamed vegetables.

Hand Only

durum semolina	1 cup
broccoli, cooked and pureed	½ cup

---

per 1-cup serving   214 calories, 8.4 g protein, 42.8 g carbohydrate, 1.0 g fat, 4.0 mg sodium

ASPARAGUS PASTA

Fresh, cooked or canned asparagus may be pureed in a food processor or blender. The asparagus provides moisture to the dough, which may require a longer kneading than usual. As the moisture content of the asparagus itself varies, watch the dough carefully for texture. If water is added too soon, by the time the kneading is completed, the dough may become too sticky. If so, simply add more flour until the proper consistency is obtained. This seemed to dry better when dusted with semolina flour and laid flat; otherwise simply cook it right away.

	Hand	Extruder
durum semolina	1 cup	1¼ cups
dry mustard, ground	⅛ tsp.	⅛ tsp.
OR ground nutmeg	¼ tsp.	¼ tsp.
asparagus puree	⅓ cup	⅓ cup
water, if and as needed	2-3 tbs.	2 tbs.

per 1-cup serving   217 calories, 8.6 g protein, 42.8 g carbohydrate, 1.3 g fat, 12.9 mg sodium

ORANGE GINGER PASTA

A flavorful pasta which goes nicely with **Orange Chicken**, *page 139,* **Orange Beef,** *page 152, or any recipe using orange juice or ginger.*

	Hand	Extruder
durum semolina	1 cup	1¼ cups
ground ginger	½ tsp.	½ tsp.
cinnamon	¼ tsp.	¼ tsp.
nutmeg	dash	dash
ground cloves	dash	dash
orange juice concentrate, thawed	¼ cup	¼ cup
vegetable oil, optional	—	1 tbs.
water, if and as needed		

per 1-cup serving   219 calories, 8.1 g protein, 44.3 g carbohydrate, 1.0 g fat, 0.2 mg sodium

CRANBERRY ORANGE PASTA

A great pasta served with a fruited chicken or as a side dish to leftover turkey!

	Hand	**Extruder**
durum semolina	1 cup	1¼ cups
cranberry juice concentrate, thawed	2 tbs.	2 tbs.
orange juice concentrate, thawed	2 tbs.	2 tbs.
vegetable oil, optional	1 tbs.	1 tbs.
water, as needed		

per 1-cup serving 255 calories, 8.0 g protein, 43.4 g carbohydrate, 5.5 g fat, 0.3 mg sodium

APPLE CINNAMON PASTA

Serve this very flavorful pasta topped with sautéed apples and raisins, herbs or chicken. Combines nicely with nutmeg pasta.

	Hand	Extruder
durum semolina	1 cup	1¼ cups
cinnamon	⅓ tsp.	½ tsp.
apple juice concentrate, thawed	¼ cup	¼ cup
vegetable oil, optional	—	1 tbs.
water, if and as needed		

per 1-cup serving   219 calories, 8.1 g protein, 44.3 g carbohydrate, 1.0 g fat, 0.2 mg sodium

APRICOT CORN PASTA

Serve this delightful pasta with an apricot or fruited chicken or seafood dish.

	Hand	Extruder
durum semolina	¾ cup	1 cup
cornmeal	¼ cup	⅓ cup
apricot nectar	¼-⅓ cup	¼-⅓ cup
vegetable or olive oil, optional	1 tbs.	1 tbs.

per 1-cup serving   299 calories, 9.0g protein, 52.6 g carbohydrate, 5.9 g fat, 32.6 mg sodium

PINEAPPLE PASTA

Serve with **Pineapple Sauce**, page 151, or with butter and freshly grated Parmesan cheese as a side dish with ham.

	Hand	**Extruder**
durum semolina	1 cup	1¼ cups
pineapple juice	¼-⅓ cup	¼-⅓ cup
ground ginger	pinch	pinch
vegetable oil, optional	—	1 tbs.

per 1-cup serving   222 calories, 8.1 g protein, 44.9 g carbohydrate, 1.0 g fat, 0.2 mg sodium

ORANGE PASTA

You only need a little butter and freshly grated Parmesan cheese tossed with this flavorful pasta.

	Hand	**Extruder**
durum semolina	1 cup	1¼ cups
orange juice	¼-⅓ cup	⅓ cup
grated orange peel	½ tsp.	½ tsp.

per 1-cup serving   219 calories, 8.1 g protein, 44.2 g carbohydrate, 1.0 g fat, 0.2 mg sodium

CRANBERRY PASTA

A delicate flavoring of cranberry in this pasta complements **Orange Cranberry Chicken**, page 142. Thaw the cranberry juice concentrate.

	Hand	**Extruder**
durum semolina	1 cup	1¼ cups
egg	1	1
cranberry juice concentrate	2-2½ tbs.	1-2 tbs.

per 1-cup serving   238 calories, 10.1 g protein, 43.0 g carbohydrate, 2.7 g fat, 21.2 mg sodium

COCONUT PASTA

A divine pasta served with **Coconut Shrimp**, page 137. This recipe was tested using unsweetened coconut milk, which is available in grocery or health food stores. I recommend this for hand machines only.

	Hand Only
durum semolina	1 cup
coconut milk	¼-⅓ cup

per 1-cup serving   247 calories, 8.4 g protein, 42.5 g carbohydrate, 5.0 g fat, 2.4 mg sodium

PUMPKIN PASTA

Fresh pumpkin which has been cooked and pureed is recommended for this pasta as it adds more moisture to the dough than canned pumpkin and works much better in extruder machines. Adjust with water or flour as necessary to achieve a proper consistency. If no pumpkin pie spice is on hand, use nutmeg or cinnamon. Make ravioli with a basic cheese sauce or pumpkin sauce for a real autumn treat.

	Hand	Extruder
durum semolina	1 cup	1¼ cups
pumpkin pie spice	dash	⅛ tsp.
pumpkin puree	¼ cup	¼ cup
vegetable oil, optional	1 tbs.	1 tbs.
water, if and as needed	1 tbs.	1-2 tbs.

per 1-cup serving   257 calories, 8.2 g protein, 43.7 g carbohydrate, 5.6 g fat, 1.0 mg sodium

POTATO PASTA

Plain potato flour may also be used for this, although it is generally more difficult to find. This basic pasta may be served with any sauce or topping.

	Hand	Extruder
durum semolina	3/4 cup	1 cup
potato starch flour	1/4 cup	1/3 cup
vegetable oil, optional	1 tbs.	1 tbs.
egg	1	1
water, if and as needed	2-3 tbs.	1-3 tbs.

per 1-cup serving   251 calories, 8.1 g protein, 38.7 g carbohydrate, 7.0 g fat, 22.3 mg sodium

GLUTEN-FREE

These recipes were devised for, but are not limited to, people who do not or cannot eat wheat. Everyone will find them to be delicious. While related to wheat, both spelt and kamut can generally be tolerated by people who have Celiac Sprue; if in doubt, check with your physician. Spelt and kamut flours work very well as direct substitutions for wheat. Spelt usually requires less water or liquid than either kamut or wheat. Recipes were tested using the flour listed.

KAMUT PASTA: BASIC GLUTEN-FREE

An ancient Egyptian grain, kamut may be eaten by many wheat-sensitive people. It is higher in protein than most wheat and may be served with any type of topping desired. Kamut absorbs water differently than wheat, so the water should be added slowly, one teaspoon at a time, until the proper consistency is obtained.

	Hand	Extruder
kamut flour	1 cup	1¼ cups
egg	1	1
vegetable or olive oil, optional	1 tbs.	1 tbs.
water, if and as needed	2-3 tbs.	2-3 tbs.

per 1-cup serving   292 calories, 11.4 g protein, 54.9 g carbohydrate, 7.5 g fat, 21.0 mg sodium

SPELT PASTA: BASIC GLUTEN-FREE

Spelt, which dates back more than 9000 years and is mentioned in the Old Testament, has a nutty, whole grain flavor and is higher in protein and some vitamins than wheat. It has a good consistency which is easy to roll; it may be slow to extrude initially but picks up speed quickly. Spelt requires less water than wheat or kamut.

	Hand	Extruder
spelt flour	1 cup	1¼ cups
egg	1	1
vegetable or olive oil, optional	1 tbs.	1 tbs.
water, if and as needed		

---

per 1-cup serving   354 calories, 12.7 g protein, 56.2 g carbohydrate, 8.9 g fat, 22.3 mg sodium

AMARANTH PASTA: BASIC GLUTEN-FREE

This pasta has a wonderful nutty flavor and may be served with any sauce. It rolls and extrudes nicely.

	Hand	Extruder
amaranth flour	2/3 cup	1 cup
tapioca flour	1/3 cup	1/4 cup
egg	1	1
vegetable or walnut oil, optional	1 tbs.	1 tbs.
water, if and as needed	1-2 tbs.	1-2 tbs.

per 1-cup serving   253 calories, 7.9 g protein, 36.7 g carbohydrate, 8.4 g fat, 25.9 mg sodium

QUINOA PASTA: BASIC GLUTEN-FREE

Quinoa has a strong, nutty taste. Top with any sauce. It is difficult to roll initially and may require several passes through the widest rollers; it extrudes nicely.

	Hand	Extruder
quinoa flour	½ cup	⅔ cup
potato starch flour	¼ cup	⅓ cup
tapioca flour	⅓ cup	⅓ cup
egg	1	1
vegetable oil, optional	1 tbs.	1 tbs.
water, if and as needed	1-2 tbs.	1-2 tbs.

per 1-cup serving   270 calories, 8.1 g protein, 41.8 g carbohydrate, 8.2 g fat, 29.9 mg sodium

QUINOA CORN PASTA

This wonderful pasta may be served with any kind of sauce or topping. It is very fragile and breaks easily during rolling and extruding. Don't roll it too thinly and use a thicker shape such as fettuccine rather than spaghetti. It holds its shape nicely during cooking.

	Hand	Extruder
quinoa flour	½ cup	⅔ cup
cornmeal	½ cup	⅔ cup
tapioca flour	⅓ cup	½ cup
egg	1	1
vegetable oil, optional	1 tbs.	1 tbs.
water, if and as needed	2-3 tbs.	1-2 tbs.

per 1-cup serving   315 calories, 9.9 g protein, 49.9 g carbohydrate, 8.9 g fat, 92.2 mg sodium

HERB SPELT PASTA

The dried herbs may be replaced with fresh, chopped herbs with the hand cranked machine — simply triple the amount. Liquid garlic juice may be used instead of the minced or pressed garlic. This very basic herb combination complements just about any food or sauce.

	Hand	Extruder
spelt flour	1 cup	1⅓ cups
oregano, dried	⅓-½ tsp.	⅓-½ tsp.
parsley, dried	⅓-½ tsp.	⅓-½ tsp.
black pepper	¼ tsp.	¼ tsp.
clove garlic, minced	1	1
egg	1	1
vegetable or olive oil, optional	1 tbs.	1 tbs.
water, if and as needed	1 tbs.	1 tbs.

per 1-cup serving   356 calories, 12.8 g protein, 56.5 g carbohydrate, 8.9 g fat, 23.1 mg sodium

MINT KAMUT PASTA

This savory pasta is wonderful served with lamb or a Greek-style dinner.

	Hand	Extruder
kamut flour	1 cup	1⅓ cups
mint, dried	1 tsp.	1¼ tsp.
OR fresh mint, chopped	1 tbs.	—
lemon pepper	½ tsp.	½ tsp.
egg	1	1
olive oil, optional	—	1 tbs.
water, if and as needed	1-3 tbs.	2 tbs.

per 1-cup serving   253 calories, 11.5 g protein, 55.1 g carbohydrate, 3.0 g fat, 21.7 mg sodium

SPICY KAMUT PASTA

This complements any number of sauces or toppings, ranging from a basic tomato to poultry or seafood with parsley or lentils. Liquid garlic juice may be used in place of the minced or pressed garlic.

	Hand	**Extruder**
kamut flour	1 cup	1¼ cups
garlic clove, minced	1	1
onion powder	⅛ tsp.	⅛ tsp.
cayenne pepper	¼ tsp.	⅓ tsp.
black pepper, coarsely ground	¼ tsp.	⅓ tsp.
parsley, dried	⅓ tsp.	⅓ tsp.
OR fresh parsley, chopped	1 tsp.	—
egg	1	1
vegetable or olive oil, optional	1 tbs.	1 tbs.
water, as needed	2-3 tbs.	2-3 tbs.

per 1-cup serving   295 calories, 11.6 g protein, 55.6 g carbohydrate, 7.6 g fat, 22.2 mg sodium

FOUR-SPICE KAMUT PASTA

This recipe contains a typical European spice blend which may be adjusted to taste and goes well with just about anything.

	Hand	Extruder
kamut flour	1 cup	1¼ cups
black pepper, coarsely ground	¼-½ tsp.	⅓-½ tsp.
ground nutmeg	⅛-¼ tsp.	⅛-¼ tsp.
ground cloves	⅛ tsp.	⅛ tsp.
ground ginger	⅛ tsp.	⅛ tsp.
egg	1	1
vegetable oil, optional	1 tbs.	1 tbs.
water, if and as needed	1-2 tbs.	1-2 tbs.

per 1-cup serving   293 calories, 11.4 g protein, 55.1 g carbohydrate, 7.6 g fat, 21.3 mg sodium

BAHARAT KAMUT PASTA

Baharat is a hot blend of spices used in Middle Eastern cooking which comple-ments the kamut nicely. This very dark brown pasta was difficult to roll in the hand machine at first, and may require several passes through the initially wide rollers.

	Hand	**Extruder**
kamut flour	1 cup	1¼ cups
chili powder	pinch	pinch
cinnamon	⅛ tsp.	⅛ tsp.
cardamom	⅛ tsp.	⅛ tsp.
nutmeg	¼ tsp.	¼ tsp.
cloves	¼ tsp.	¼ tsp.
black pepper	¼ tsp.	¼ tsp.
coriander	¼ tsp.	¼ tsp.
cumin	¼ tsp.	¼ tsp.
paprika	½ tsp.	½ tsp.
egg	1	1
vegetable oil, optional	1 tbs.	1 tbs.
water, if and as needed	2-3 tbs.	2-3 tbs.

per 1-cup serving   296 calories, 11.6 g protein, 55.6 g carbohydrate, 7.7 g fat, 22.6 mg sodium

LEMON PASTA: GLUTEN-FREE

Lemon pasta complements any fish or seafood with lemon or any sauce or topping using spinach and/or lemon.

	Hand	Extruder
kamut flour	1 cup	1⅓ cups
oregano, dried	1 tsp.	1 tsp.
OR fresh oregano, chopped	1 tbs.	—
vegetable oil, optional	—	1 tbs.
egg	1	1
lemon juice	2 tbs.	2 tbs.
water, if needed		

per 1-cup serving 256 calories, 11.5 g protein, 55.9 g carbohydrate, 3.1 g fat, 23.2 mg sodium

VARIATIONS

- **Lemon Pepper:** Omit oregano and use 1 tsp. of coarsely ground black pepper.

- **Lemon Pepper Chive:** Add 1-1½ tsp. dried chives to *Lemon Pepper*.

- **Lemon Dill:** Omit the oregano and use 1 tsp. dill weed.

- **Lemon Rosemary:** Omit the oregano and use 1 tsp. rosemary leaves.

KAMUT PARSLEY PEPPER PASTA

Parsley pepper complements a wide variety of foods from Italian to Mexican. It is a nice dish by itself with butter and Parmesan cheese or it may accompany any fish, seafood, beef, tomato or cheese sauce or topping.

	Hand	Extruder
kamut flour	1 cup	1¼ cups
black pepper, coarsely ground	½-1 tsp.	½-1 tsp.
parsley, dried	1-2 tsp.	1-2 tsp.
OR fresh parsley, chopped	1-2 tbs.	—
vegetable oil, optional	1 tbs.	1 tbs.
water	¼-⅓ cup	¼-⅓ cup

per 1-cup serving   269 calories, 9.5 g protein, 55.1 g carbohydrate, 5.9 g fat, 2.7 mg sodium

KAMUT BASIL OREGANO PASTA

This is great with any tomato-based sauce or meal.

	Hand	Extruder
kamut flour	1 cup	1¼ cups
basil, dried	1 tsp.	1 tsp.
OR fresh basil, chopped	1 tbs.	—
oregano, dried	1 tsp.	1 tsp.
OR fresh oregano, chopped	1 tbs.	—
black pepper, optional	½-1 tsp.	½-1 tsp.
vegetable oil, optional	1 tbs.	1 tbs.
water, if and as needed	¼-⅓ cup	¼-⅓ cup

per 1-cup serving   274 calories, 9.7 g protein, 56.7 g carbohydrate, 6.1 g fat, 1.7 mg sodium

TOMATO BASIL PASTA: GLUTEN-FREE

This is a superb pasta with any tomato-based sauce. For real eye appeal, try combining this with spinach pasta.

	Hand	**Extruder**
kamut flour	1 cup	1¼ cups
basil, dried	1 tsp.	1 tsp.
OR fresh basil, chopped	1 tbs.	—
tomato juice	⅓-½ cup	⅓-½ cup

per 1-cup serving   235 calories, 9.8 g protein, 56.7 g carbohydrate, 1.4 g fat, 81.2 mg sodium

SPINACH PASTA: GLUTEN-FREE

Cook and drain the chopped spinach, reserving the liquid in case more moisture is required for the dough. This may be difficult to roll out the first time through a hand-cranked machine. Simply repeat the process using the rollers at the widest point until it rolls through smoothly. Don't be too quick to add water to the dough in the extruder as moisture is obtained from the spinach itself during both the kneading and extruding. If dough becomes too sticky in the extruder, add a little more flour to mix if your machine allows or dust with flour as it extrudes to prevent sticking. This recipe may be difficult to work at first but results in a flavorful spinach pasta.

	Hand	Extruder
kamut flour	1 cup	1¼ cups
chopped spinach, cooked	⅓ cup	⅓ cup
lemon pepper	1 tsp.	1 tsp.

per 1-cup serving   233 calories, 10.0 g protein, 55.9 g carbohydrate, 1.4 g fat, 14.2 mg sodium

SAUCES, TOPPINGS AND FILLINGS

This book is not meant to be a comprehensive book on sauces with which to serve the pasta; rather it is intended to provide a variety of pasta recipes, and a few basic and complementary sauces.

Pasta can be used as the basis for a main meal or as a side dish. For example, the flavorful pastas found in the *Herb and Spice* chapter make wonderful side dishes tossed with softened butter, olive oil or even with a salad dressing, and perhaps the addition of a grated cheese. Try one of the flavored olive oils carried in many grocery and gourmet stores.

The flavor of the pasta should complement the sauce or meal with which it is served. You now have more than 100 new and exciting pasta recipes from which to choose the perfect accompaniment to your favorite meal. Let the sauces and toppings in this chapter serve as a springboard for your imagination and don't be afraid to experiment or to make substitutions!

There are any number of items which may be in the garden, refrigerator or on cabinet shelves which may be thrown together for delicious pasta toppings. The following list offers ideas to stimulate thinking:

- Cheeses, freshly grated. Parmesan cheese is often used, but consider soft cheeses that melt easily, Monterey Jack with or without jalapeño peppers, Feta, Gorgonzola (spicy) or provolone (for baking) and ricotta (for stuffing).

- Freshly chopped tomatoes, diced mushrooms and/or other fresh vegetables

- Any steamed vegetables, fresh or frozen

- Vegetables such as zucchini, yellow squash, or tomato slices sautéed in olive oil with basil or other herbs

- Fruits such as grapes, apples, orange segments, and yogurt

- Beans or lentils (and onions) for complete protein

- Any leftover meats or meals

- Nuts such as walnuts or pine nuts (pignoli), sautéed in a little olive oil, tossed with grated cheese and/or vegetables

- Canned shrimp, crab, tuna or salmon; canned meats

Canned Italian tomatoes or stewed tomatoes are used in many recipes. If you prefer to use fresh tomatoes, here are two recipes. Drop tomatoes into boiling water for 1 to 2 minutes, followed by ice water for 30 seconds, and the skin will come off easily. One 14 oz. can equals approximately 1½-1¾ cups of home-prepared tomatoes.

STEWED TOMATOES

4 large tomatoes or 6-7 Italian plum tomatoes
1 tbs. onion, finely diced or 1 tsp. dried minced onion
¼ cup diced celery

2-3 tbs. diced bell peppers
1½ tsp. sugar
½ tsp. salt, optional
parsley or basil to taste, optional

Wash, skin and halve or quarter tomatoes. Place all ingredients in a saucepan, cover and simmer over low heat, stirring occasionally for 20 to 30 minutes.

COOKED ITALIAN TOMATOES

10-12 Italian plum tomatoes

salt and/or basil to taste

Wash, skin and halve tomatoes. Add seasoning, place in a saucepan, cover and simmer over low heat, stirring occasionally for 15 to 20 minutes.

BASIC CREAM (ALFREDO) SAUCE

The seasonings which may be added to this basic cream sauce are limited only by your imagination. Try them alone or in combination. If tossing with an herb pasta, try the same basic herbs in the cream sauce!

6 tbs. butter
3/4 cup heavy cream
4-5 oz. grated Parmesan cheese
salt and white pepper to taste

1/4 tsp. garlic powder, optional
1/2-1 tsp. Italian seasonings, basil, oregano, mint, poppy seeds, parsley flakes, jalapeño flakes, optional

Melt butter in a large skillet and add cream, stirring until well blended. Add cheese slowly, stirring constantly until desired consistency is obtained. Use less cheese for a thinner, lighter sauce and more for a thicker, heavier sauce.

Serve with: Fettuccine of any variety
Servings: This single recipe may be tossed with 1/2 lb. of pasta for a heavy cheese sauce to feed 3-4 or with 1 lb. of pasta for a light cheese sauce to feed 6-8 people.

per 1/8 recipe   222 calories, 6.3 g protein, 1.2 g carbohydrate, 21.7 g fat, 361 mg sodium

PRIMAVERA

Primavera is made from any fresh vegetable and may include any of your favorites such as peas, cauliflower, string beans, and others. For a spicier primavera, add a little crushed red pepper to taste.

1-2 stalks broccoli florets
1 medium yellow squash or 2 small, sliced
1 medium zucchini or 2 small, sliced
4-6 tbs. butter
1/4-1/2 cup onion, diced

1-2 cloves garlic, minced or pressed
salt and pepper to taste
3/4 cup heavy cream
4-5 oz. freshly grated Parmesan cheese

Steam or boil broccoli, yellow squash and zucchini until just tender but not yet completely cooked, and set aside. Sauté onion and garlic in butter until soft. Add cream and cheese to onion mixture, stirring constantly until well blended and cheese melts. Add steamed vegetables and toss with pasta.

Serve with: Any vegetable or grain pasta, *Three Pepper Pasta*
Servings: 3-4 with 1/2 lb. of pasta or 6-8 with 1 lb. of pasta

per 1/8 recipe   207 calories, 7.1 g protein, 3.7 g carbohydrate, 18.7 g fat, 335 mg sodium

SHRIMP DILL SAUCE

For a low fat version, cook the vegetables in a little chicken broth instead of butter. Substitute chervil, basil or oregano for the dill and serve with complementary pasta.

1 lb. raw shrimp
1 tbs. butter or margarine or use
  vegetable spray
1/4 cup finely diced red onion
1-2 cloves of garlic, minced or
  pressed, optional

1/4 cup finely diced green or red bell
  pepper
1/3-1/2 cup chicken broth or bouillon
1 tbs. arrowroot powder or cornstarch
1 1/2 tsp. dill weed
salt and pepper to taste

Shell and devein shrimp and set aside. Sauté vegetables in butter until soft. Stir arrowroot or cornstarch into cold chicken broth or bouillon and add all remaining ingredients. Simmer until shrimp turns pink and is done, about 5 to 10 minutes. Toss with hot pasta and serve immediately.

Serve with: *Dilly Pasta*
Servings: 3

per 1/3 recipe   190 calories, 32.6 g protein, 12.8 g carbohydrate, 3.0 g fat, 485 mg sodium

GREEK SHRIMP

Try this garnished with crumbled Feta cheese.

2 tbs. olive oil
¼ cup lemon juice
1-2 cloves minced garlic
¼ cup onion, finely diced
1 bay leaf

2 tsp. dried parsley or 2 tbs. fresh, chopped parsley
salt and pepper to taste
1 lb. raw shrimp, shelled and deveined

Mix all ingredients together in a large skillet and cook over medium heat covered, stirring occasionally until shrimp are pink and done, about 5 to 10 minutes. Remove bay leaf, toss with hot pasta and serve immediately.

Serve with: Any lemon pasta
Servings: 3

VARIATIONS

- Use black or lemon pepper.

- Substitute 1 lb. of boneless chicken, diced.

per ⅓ recipe   228 calories, 31.2 g protein, 5.0 g carbohydrate, 12.1 g fat, 235 mg sodium

COCONUT SHRIMP

Garnish with shredded coconut if desired.

1 lb. raw shrimp
½ bell pepper, diced
¼ cup finely diced onion
1 tbs. olive oil
⅔ cup coconut milk, unsweetened

1 egg
½-1 tsp. cilantro, dried or
  ½-1 tbs. fresh cilantro, chopped
salt and pepper to taste

Shell and devein shrimp. Sauté shrimp, pepper and onion in oil until shrimp are pink and onions are golden brown, about 5 to 10 minutes. Add remaining ingredients and cook over medium heat, stirring occasionally until it thickens.

Serve with: Any coconut, southwestern or Mexican pasta
Servings: 3

VARIATIONS
- Substitute oregano or parsley for the cilantro.

---

per ⅓ recipe   360 calories, 34.8 g protein, 17.5 g carbohydrate, 19.8 g fat, 259 mg sodium

CAJUN SHRIMP

This spicy dish is a perfect choice when you have guests.

1-2 tbs. butter
½ medium onion, diced
1-2 cloves garlic, minced
1 red or green bell pepper, diced
1 stalk celery, sliced
1 can (14 oz.) stewed tomatoes
¼ cup white wine

2-3 drops Tabasco Sauce, or to taste
½ tsp. salt
¼ tsp. coarsely ground black pepper
½ tsp. celery seed
1 tsp. thyme
1½ tbs. parsley
1 lb. shrimp, shelled and deveined

Melt butter in a large skillet and sauté vegetables until soft. Add tomatoes, wine, Tabasco and seasonings. Simmer over low heat, stirring occasionally for about 45 minutes. Add shrimp and cook until shrimp are pink, about 5 to 10 minutes.

Serve with: *Cajun, Pepper, Parsley Pepper Pasta*
Servings: 2-3

VARIATION

● Substitute chicken or turkey for shrimp.

per ⅓ recipe   236 calories, 33.1 g protein, 13.9 g carbohydrate, 7.4 g fat, 952 mg sodium

ORANGE CHICKEN

Garnish with mandarin orange sections if desired.

MARINADE

1 tbs. soy sauce
1 tsp. sesame oil
1 tbs. rice vinegar
2 tbs. orange juice concentrate, thawed
1 tsp. brown sugar

1 lb. boneless chicken breasts, diced
1 tbs. arrowroot powder or cornstarch

1-2 cloves garlic, minced
1/4 tsp. ginger powder or
   1/2 tsp. minced fresh ginger root
1 tsp. orange peel
salt, crushed red pepper flakes to taste

1/4 cup orange juice

Mix marinade ingredients together. Place chicken in mixture and marinate for several hours in the refrigerator. Cook chicken with marinade mixture in a skillet over medium heat until chicken is lightly browned. Combine arrowroot or cornstarch with orange juice until dissolved. Add to skillet and heat until sauce is heated throughout and thickens. Serve over or tossed with hot pasta.

Serve with: *Orange Pasta, Sesame Pasta, Ginger Pasta, Orange Ginger Pasta*
Servings: 2-3

per 1/3 recipe 223 calories, 24.1 g protein, 8.9 g carbohydrate, 3.5 g fat, 452 mg sodium

SWEET AND SOUR PINEAPPLE CHICKEN

This is delicious, and quick and easy, too!

MARINADE
½ cup pineapple juice
2 tbs. honey
3 tbs. soy sauce
½ tsp. orange peel
salt and pepper to taste

1 lb. boneless chicken breasts, diced

Mix marinade ingredients together, add chicken and marinate for at least 1 hour in the refrigerator. Cook chicken and marinade over medium heat in a skillet until chicken is lightly browned.

Serve with: *Pineapple Pasta, Coconut Pasta, Orange Pasta*
Servings: 2-3

---

per ⅓ recipe 250 calories, 24.9 g protein, 18.8 g carbohydrate, 2.0 g fat, 1150 mg sodium

GREEK CHICKEN

Good with any lemon pasta — lemon pepper is great!

1 lb. boneless chicken breast, diced
1-2 tbs. olive oil
1/4 cup finely chopped onion
1-2 cloves garlic, minced
1 can (14½ oz.) stewed tomatoes

salt and pepper to taste
1 tsp. cinnamon
2 tsp. dried parsley or 2 tbs. fresh
   chopped parsley
2 tbs. lemon juice

In a large skillet, cook chicken in olive oil until browned. Add onions and cook until golden and soft. Add remaining ingredients, cover and simmer over low heat for approximately 30 minutes.

Serve with: Any lemon pasta such as *Lemon Pepper Pasta*
Servings: 2-3

VARIATION
• Substitute lemon pepper for black pepper.

per ⅓ recipe   257 calories, 25.1 g protein, 10.1 g carbohydrate, 7.2 g fat, 403 mg sodium

ORANGE CRANBERRY CHICKEN

This is a great use for leftover chicken or turkey.

2 cups diced, cooked chicken
1/3 cup orange juice
1 can (11 oz.) mandarin orange
  segments, drained
1 cup fresh cranberries

1 tbs. brown sugar
salt and pepper to taste
1/4 cup orange juice
1 tbs. cornstarch

Combine chicken, orange juice, orange segments, cranberries, brown sugar and seasonings in a medium saucepan, cover and simmer for approximately 15 to 20 minutes. Blend cornstarch into orange juice and add to other ingredients, stirring until mixture thickens.

Serve with: *Cranberry Pasta* and/or *Orange Pasta*
Servings: 2-3

per 1/3 recipe   201 calories, 10.6 g protein, 33.8 g carbohydrate, 1.1 g fat, 40.2 mg sodium

GINGER CILANTRO CHICKEN

Add 1 or 2 cups of diced vegetables such as snow peas, broccoli or bell peppers as you are cooking the meat, or steam the vegetables and toss in with the sauce and pasta.

1/3 cup soy sauce
2 tbs. sesame oil
1 tbs. rice vinegar
1/2 inch ginger root, finely diced
1 tbs. dried cilantro or 3 tbs. fresh
  chopped cilantro

1/4 medium red onion, diced
1-2 cloves garlic, minced
1 lb. boneless chicken breast, cut
  into bite-sized pieces

Mix all ingredients together and let chicken marinate in the refrigerator for several hours. Cook in a large skillet or wok over low heat until chicken is cooked. Toss with pasta and serve immediately.

Serve with: *Mexican Herb Pasta, Ginger Pasta* or *Sesame Pasta*
Servings: 3 (more with vegetables)

---

per 1/3 recipe   283 calories, 26.1 g protein, 5.1 g carbohydrate, 11.0 g fat, 1850 mg sodium

BASIC TOMATO SAUCE

I do not use any additional oil when browning meat — but you may choose to. The amount of tomato paste you use depends on the desired thickness of the sauce.

½ lb. ground turkey and/or beef
½ lb. Italian sausage, diced
½ cup onion, finely diced
1-2 cloves garlic, minced
1 can (28 oz.) Italian tomatoes, quartered, or 2 cans (15 oz. each)
1 can (14½ oz.) stewed tomatoes

1-2 tbs. tomato paste
1 tbs. dried oregano or 3 tbs. chopped fresh oregano, or to taste
2 tsp. dried basil or 2 tbs. chopped fresh basil, or to taste
crushed red pepper to taste, optional
salt and pepper to taste

Cook meat in a large skillet until well browned. Remove meat to a large saucepan and cook onion and garlic in skillet until soft. Mix all remaining ingredients in saucepan, cover and simmer for about an hour, stirring occasionally. Adjust seasonings to taste. Meat may be omitted if desired.

Serve with: Any basic grain or flavorful herb pasta - goes with almost everything
Servings: 4-6 with 1 lb. (2 recipes) of pasta

per ⅙ recipe   242 calories, 14.7 g protein, 13.5 g carbohydrate, 14.9 g fat, 866 mg sodium

GREEK SPAGHETTI SAUCE

As with any tomato sauce recipe, you can use fresh tomatoes: see page 132.

1 lb. ground turkey and/or beef
1/2 cup finely diced onion
1 garlic, minced
1 can (28 oz.) Italian tomatoes,
  quartered
2 tsp. cinnamon

1/4 tsp. nutmeg
1/2 tsp. salt
1/3 tsp. black pepper
1 tsp. dried parsley or 1 tbs.
  chopped fresh parsley

Brown meat in a large skillet over medium heat. Remove to a saucepan with a slotted spoon. Sauté onion and garlic in remaining liquid until lightly brown and soft. Drain liquid. Add onions, garlic and remaining ingredients to meat. Simmer over low heat for 45 to 60 minutes until sauce begins to thicken. Adjust seasonings to taste. Meat may be omitted if desired.

Serve with: *Cinnamon Pasta, Garlic Parsley Pasta, Nutmeg Pasta*
Servings: 4-6 with 1 lb. of pasta (2 recipes)

---

per 1/6 recipe   117 calories, 8.2 g protein, 8.6 g carbohydrate, 6.1 g fat, 510 mg sodium

SCARBOROUGH TOMATO SAUCE

For a low fat version, sauté the onions in a nonstick pan or one that has been coated with vegetable spray.

1 can (28 oz.) Italian tomatoes, smashed with a fork
1/4 cup onion, finely diced
1-2 cloves garlic, minced
1 tbs. dried parsley or 3 tbs. chopped fresh parsley

1 tsp. sage
1 tsp. rosemary
1 tsp. thyme
1/4-1/2 tsp. salt
1/2 tsp. coarsely ground black pepper

Combine all ingredients in a medium saucepan and simmer over low heat for 20 to 30 minutes. Stir occasionally.

Serve with: *Scarborough "Fare" Pasta*
Servings: 4-6 with 1 lb. (2 recipes) of pasta
VARIATIONS

- Add 1 lb. cooked ground meat (beef or turkey) and onions.

- See page 132 for directions about using fresh tomatoes.

per 1/6 recipe   39.9 calories, 1.8 g protein, 8.7 g carbohydrate, 0.5 g fat, 393 mg sodium

MEXICAN TOMATO SAUCE

You can substitute 1 lb. cooked ground meat with taco seasoning for the beans, and cayenne pepper or chili powder for the red pepper flakes.

1 tbs. olive oil
1/4-1/3 cup finely diced onion
1-2 cloves garlic, minced
1 can (28 oz.) Italian-style tomatoes
1 cup salsa

1 can (16 oz.) black beans, rinsed, drained or 8 oz. dry beans soaked overnight, drained
1 tsp. dried basil or 1 tbs. chopped fresh basil
1/2-1 tsp. crushed red pepper
salt and pepper to taste

In a large saucepan, cook onion and garlic in oil until soft. Add remaining ingredients and simmer over low heat for 30 to 45 minutes.

Serve with: *Spicy Southwestern, Jalapeño, Mexican Herb, Red Pepper, Three Pepper, Cinnamon, Southwestern Corn Pastas*

Servings: 4-6 with 1 lb. (2 recipes) of pasta

per 1/6 recipe   171 calories, 7.3 g protein, 24.2 g carbohydrate, 3.1 g fat, 1148 mg sodium

INDONESIAN PEANUT SAUCE

A great accompaniment to a grilled chicken meal, as the sauce can be used for both the pasta and chicken! Or if desired, simply toss some cooked chicken in with the pasta and sauce.

⅓ cup peanut butter
½ cup coconut milk, unsweetened
⅓ cup chicken broth or bouillon
½ tsp. crushed red pepper
½-1 tsp. jalapeño flakes or
  ½-1 jalapeño, minced
1-2 cloves garlic, minced

⅛ tsp. ground ginger or ½ tsp.
  minced fresh ginger root
1 tsp. soy sauce
2-3 drops Tabasco Sauce or
  Mongolian Fire Oil
salt and pepper to taste

Mix all ingredients in a food processor and toss with hot pasta.

Serve with: *Coconut* or *Ginger Pasta*
Servings: 3 (more with meat)

---

per ⅓ recipe   245 calories, 9.4 g protein, 6.9 g carbohydrate, 22.0 g fat, 379 mg sodium

SPICY BLACK BEANS

You can use cayenne pepper instead of crushed red pepper.

1 tbs. vegetable oil
¼ cup diced red onion
1-2 cloves garlic, minced
1 can (15 oz.) black beans, rinsed
  and drained
1 can (11 oz.) mandarin orange
  segments, rinsed and drained

1 tbs. lime juice
¼ cup orange juice
1 tbs. dried cilantro or 3 tbs. fresh
  chopped cilantro
crushed red pepper and salt to taste

In a large skillet, sauté onion and garlic in oil until soft. Add remaining ingredients and simmer over low heat for approximately 1 hour, stirring occasionally until sauce thickens. Toss with hot pasta and serve immediately.

Serve with: *Mexican Herb Pasta, Salsa Pasta, Orange Pasta*
Servings: 2-3

per ⅓ *recipe*   286 calories, 12.5 g protein, 44.4 g carbohydrate, 5.4 g fat, 525 mg sodium

BLACK BEAN SAUCE

This may also be used as a dip with chips if you melt the cheese with the other ingredients.

1 can (15 oz.) black beans, rinsed and drained
1 cup salsa
1-2 cloves garlic, minced
½ tsp. dried cilantro or 1½ tsp. chopped fresh cilantro, optional
¼ cup diced red onion
1 green onion, chopped
salt and cayenne pepper to taste
1 cup shredded cheddar cheese

Combine all ingredients except cheese in a large skillet and simmer over low heat until warm. Add cheese until it melts and toss with pasta, or toss sauce with pasta and top with cheese.

Serve with: *Spicy Southwestern, Jalapeño, Mexican Herb, Southwestern Corn, Corn, Amaranth Pastas*
Servings: 3-4

per ¼ recipe 278 calories, 15.9 g protein, 26.5 g carbohydrate, 9.9 g fat, 902 mg sodium

PINEAPPLE SAUCE

This sauce with pasta is good served with cooked or grilled shrimp, chicken or ham.

1 can (8 oz.) crushed pineapple with juice
1 tsp. soy sauce
1 tbs. brown sugar
¼ tsp. ground ginger
2 tbs. cold water
1 tsp. cornstarch

Mix pineapple, juice, soy sauce, brown sugar and ginger together and simmer over low heat while preparing pasta. Dissolve cornstarch in water and add to warm ingredients, stirring until sauce thickens.

Serve with: *Pineapple* or *Coconut Pasta*
Servings: 2-3

---

per ⅓ recipe 73 calories, 0.5 g protein, 18.7 g carbohydrate, 0.1 g fat, 119 mg sodium

ORANGE BEEF

The combination of beef, seasonings and orange juice make a terrific meal.

1½ lbs. beef round, stew beef or
  boneless chuck, cubed
1-2 tbs. olive oil
1-2 cloves garlic, minced
¼-½ cup diced onion
¼ cup grated carrot
½ cup orange juice
1 cup beef bouillon or stock

1 bay leaf
½ tsp. caraway or anise seed
½ tsp. orange peel
1½ tsp. brown sugar
½ tsp. black pepper
¼ tsp. salt or to taste
¼ cup water
2 tbs. arrowroot powder or cornstarch

In a large skillet, brown meat in olive oil. Remove meat to a large saucepan or Dutch oven. Add onion, garlic and carrot to skillet and cook until soft. Add vegetables, juice, bouillon and seasonings to beef, cover and simmer over low heat for approximately 2 hours. About 10 minutes before serving, dissolve arrowroot in water and add to other ingredients, stirring occasionally until the sauce thickens. Remove bay leaf before serving.

Serve with: *Rye, Cornmeal Rye, Black Bean* or *Orange Pasta*
Servings: 3-4

per ¼ recipe   374 calories, 39.0 g protein, 11.6 g carbohydrate, 19.0 g fat, 426 mg sodium

PESTO

It is imperative to use fresh herbs for pesto — dried herbs don't work! To reduce fat, cut amounts of both the nuts and oil in half.

1 cup fresh basil leaves, tightly packed
2-3 cloves garlic
1/4 cup freshly grated Parmesan cheese

1/4 cup pine nuts
salt and pepper to taste
1/4 cup olive oil

Process basil, garlic, Parmesan cheese, pine nuts, salt and pepper in a food processor or blender until finely chopped and blended. While blender or processor is running, slowly add oil until blended and absorbed.

Serve with: Any grain pasta
Servings: 3-4

VARIATIONS

- Substitute walnuts, roasted macadamias or hazelnuts for the pine nuts.

- Substitute fresh mint or parsley for the basil.

---

per 1/4 recipe   270 calories, 10.2 g protein, 13.0 g carbohydrate, 23.8 g fat, 267 mg sodium

BROCCOLI PESTO

Serve this tossed with pasta and freshly steamed vegetables. Adjust seasoning to your taste.

1 stalk broccoli, cooked
1-2 cloves garlic
¼ cup freshly grated Parmesan cheese
¼ cup pine nuts or walnuts
salt and pepper to taste
½-1 tsp. crushed red pepper or ¼-½ tsp. cayenne pepper
¼ cup olive oil

Process broccoli, garlic, Parmesan cheese, pine nuts and seasonings in a food processor or blender until finely chopped and blended. While blender or processor is running, slowly add oil until blended and absorbed.

Serve with: Any grain pasta
Servings: 3-4

per ¼ recipe   205 calories, 5.4 g protein, 4.0 g carbohydrate, 20.1 g fat, 106 mg sodium

CILANTRO PESTO

You can substitute crushed red pepper for black pepper. Outstanding pesto!

1 cup fresh cilantro leaves, tightly packed
2-3 cloves garlic
¼ cup grated Parmesan cheese
¼ cup pine nuts or walnuts
¼ tsp. cinnamon
salt and pepper to taste
¼ cup olive oil

Process cilantro, garlic, Parmesan cheese, pine nuts and seasonings in a food processor or blender until finely chopped and blended. While blender or processor is running, slowly add oil until blended and absorbed.

Serve with: *Spicy Southwestern, Jalapeño, Mexican Herb, Southwestern Corn, Corn, Amaranth Pastas*
Servings: 3-4

per ¼ recipe   241 calories, 7.7 g protein, 10.1 g carbohydrate, 21.1 g fat, 166 mg sodium

SPICY ORANGE BEEF

The same basic sauce may be made and served with cooked chicken or shrimp. Sauté vegetables and simmer all ingredients for 30 minutes over low heat. Add 1 tablespoon of cornstarch or arrowroot powder mixed with ¼ cup orange juice at the end to thicken.

1-2 tbs. vegetable oil
1 lb. beef round cut into 1-inch cubes, or stew beef
1 tbs. vegetable oil
1 green or red bell pepper, sliced or diced
¼ cup diced red onion
1 clove garlic, minced
1 jalapeño pepper, seeded, finely chopped or equivalent canned
¼-½ tsp. crushed red pepper
1 cup orange juice
¼ cup white wine or water
1 tsp. dried cilantro or 1 tbs. fresh cilantro, chopped, optional
salt and pepper to taste
¼-½ cup sour cream

In a large skillet, brown meat in oil and set aside in a large saucepan or Dutch oven. Add pepper, onion, garlic, jalapeño pepper and crushed red pepper to skillet and sauté until vegetables are soft. Add vegetables to meat with orange juice, wine, cilantro, salt and pepper. Simmer over low heat for 2 hours, stirring occasionally. Just before serving, mix in sour cream and toss with pasta. Serve immediately.

Serve with: *Orange, Southwestern, Jalapeño Pastas*
Servings: 4-6 with two recipes of pasta (1 lb.)

---

per ⅙ recipe   202 calories, 18.3 g protein, 6.8 g carbohydrate, 10.3 g fat, 67.9 mg sodium

---

BEEF STROGANOFF

This may be made a day or two in advance and heated prior to serving.

1-2 tbs. melted butter or vegetable
  oil
½ lb. mushrooms, sliced
¼ cup finely diced onion
1-2 cloves garlic, minced
1-1½ lbs. beef round or rump,
  cut into 1-inch pieces, or stew beef

2-3 tbs. all purpose flour
2 cups beef stock or bouillon
½ tsp. celery seed
salt and pepper to taste
¼-½ cup sour cream

In a large skillet, sauté mushrooms, onions and garlic in butter until soft. Remove from pan and place in a large Dutch oven or saucepan. In the same skillet, brown meat, adding more butter only if necessary. Sprinkle flour over meat and transfer meat and drippings to Dutch oven. Add stock and seasonings. Simmer over low heat for about 2 hours. Just before serving, mix in sour cream and toss with pasta.

Serve with: Any basic grain pasta, *Spicy Herb Pasta, Parsley Herb Pasta*
Serves: 4-6 with two recipes of pasta (1 lb.)

per ⅙ recipe 164 calories, 19.1 g protein, 3.3 g carbohydrate, 7.8 g fat, 321 mg sodium

GARLIC PEPPER SAUCE

Add diced vegetables or leftover meats to stretch the meal.

2 tbs. olive oil
2-3 garlic cloves, minced or pressed
½-1 tsp. crushed red pepper
1-2 tsp. dried parsley or 1-2 tbs. fresh parsley, chopped

Sauté garlic and pepper in oil until garlic is golden. Toss with pasta and parsley.

Serve with: Any basic grain pasta or one which contains garlic
Servings: 2-3

---

per ⅓ recipe   84.8 calories, 0.3 g protein, 1.1 g carbohydrate, 9.4 g fat, 2.8 mg sodium

SAUTÉED WALNUTS

This is another pasta dish that can be made into a one-dish meal with the addition of vegetables and leftover meat or chicken.

2-3 tbs. olive oil
1-2 garlic cloves, minced or pressed
¼ cup chopped walnuts
¼ cup grated Parmesan cheese
1 tsp. dried parsley or basil or 1 tbs. chopped fresh parsley or basil

Sauté garlic in oil until garlic is golden. Add walnuts and sauté 1 to 2 minutes. Toss with pasta, cheese and parsley or basil.

Serve with: Any basic grain or herb pasta
Servings: 2-3

per ⅓ recipe 176 calories, 5.5 g protein, 2.1 g carbohydrate, 17.2 g. fat, 126 mg sodium

LEMON CREAM

This pasta and sauce combination is delicious with seafood. Add vegetables if you wish.

½ cup cream
1-1½ tbs. lemon juice
1 tsp. lemon peel
¼ cup grated Parmesan cheese

Mix together cream, lemon juice and lemon peel in a small saucepan and simmer over low heat until just warmed. Add cheese slowly, stirring until well blended and melted. Toss with pasta and serve immediately.

Serve with: Any lemon pasta
Servings: 2-3

per ⅓ recipe   169 calories, 3.6 g protein, 1.7 g carbohydrate, 16.7 g fat, 140 mg sodium

WALNUT CHEESE SAUCE

Omit the cream and use for a ravioli filling.

¼ cup chopped walnuts
1 tbs. vegetable oil
1 cup ricotta cheese (part-skim)
½ cup cream
¼ cup chopped fresh parsley,
1 garlic clove, minced or pressed
salt to taste

Sauté walnuts in oil for a minute or two. Combine all ingredients in a food processor and process until smooth. Heat in microwave or on stovetop until just warm and toss with hot pasta. Serve immediately.

Serve with: Any basic grain pasta or one which uses parsley
Servings: 2-3

per ⅓ recipe   323 calories, 5.8 g protein, 12.5 g carbohydrate, 27.1 g fat, 127 mg sodium

BASIC CHEESE FILLING

This basic cheese filling may be used for either lasagna or ravioli. It is enough for about 4 dozen ravioli or for one 9x13-inch pan of lasagna. Should you ever have any leftovers, refrigerate and toss with pasta another day. Select a combination of herbs to mix with the cheese and egg which will complement the pasta and/or the sauce with which it is served. If using fresh herbs, simply triple the amount given. Seasonings may be adjusted to taste if desired.

1 egg
15 oz. ricotta cheese, skim

ITALIAN FILLING

1 tbs. dried oregano or 3 tbs.
  chopped fresh oregano
2 tsp. dried parsley or 2 tbs.
  chopped fresh parsley

1 tsp. dried basil or 1 tbs. chopped
  fresh basil leaves
salt and pepper to taste

MEXICAN FILLING

2 tsp.-1 tbs. dried cilantro or 2-3 tbs.
  chopped fresh cilantro
½ tsp. crushed red pepper flakes

½ tsp. jalapeño pepper flakes or 1-2
  finely diced, seeded jalapeño peppers

GARLIC BASIL FILLING
1-2 cloves garlic, minced or pressed   1-2 tsp. dried basil

LEMON ROSEMARY (OR MINT OR BASIL) FILLING
1/2-1 tsp. lemon peel   dash salt
1-1 1/2 tsp. rosemary leaves, crushed
   OR mint or crushed basil

LEMON PARSLEY PEPPER FILLING
1 tsp. lemon peel   1/2 tsp. coarsely ground black pepper
1-2 tsp. dried parsley

VARIATIONS
- Many of the same basic herb and spice combinations which are used in the pasta itself may be mixed into this basic cheese filling.

- **Herb Butter or Yogurt:** Use these same basic herb combinations and mix into 1/2 cup softened butter or yogurt for a quick and easy topping to toss with hot pasta.

MEXICAN LASAGNA

Use any jalapeño, corn or spicy pasta made into lasagna noodles for this. For a real treat, use three different kinds and alternate layers.

1½ recipes pasta
2-3 cups of salsa or *Mexican Tomato Sauce*, page 147, or a combination
Mexican Filling, page 163
½ cup shredded mozzarella cheese
½ cup shredded Monterey Jack cheese with jalapeño peppers

Cook pasta noodles until tender but not quite done. Rinse with cold water and set aside. Place 2 or 3 spoonfuls of salsa or tomato sauce on the bottom of a 9x13-inch pan, layer lasagna noodles on top of sauce and then add enough cheese filling to lightly cover noodles. Spread meat or beans and salsa or tomato sauce on top of that. Repeat this pattern until you have 3 layers. Top with cheese and bake uncovered in a 375° oven for 30 to 40 minutes or a 350° oven for 40 to 50 minutes.

Servings: 5-6

GREEK LASAGNA

Use **Lemon, Cinnamon** or **Parsley Pepper Pasta**. Plan on about ½ lb. (1 recipe) for the pasta.

1 recipe pasta
2-3 cups of *Greek Spaghetti Sauce*, page 145
Cheese Filling, page 163
1 pkg. (10 oz.) frozen chopped spinach, cooked and drained
4 oz. Feta cheese, crumbled
1 cup shredded mozzarella cheese

Cook pasta noodles until tender but not quite done. Rinse with cold water and set aside. Place 2 or 3 spoonfuls of spaghetti sauce on the bottom of a 9x13-inch pan, layer lasagna noodles on top of sauce and then add enough cheese filling to lightly cover noodles. Spread crumbled Feta cheese and mozzarella cheese on top and bake uncovered in a 375° oven for 30 to 40 minutes or a 350° oven for 40 to 50 minutes.

Servings: 5-6

INDEX

SERVE CREATIVE, EASY, NUTRITIOUS MEALS WITH NITTY GRITTY® COOKBOOKS

Convection Oven Cookery
The Steamer Cookbook
The Pasta Machine Cookbook
The Versatile Rice Cooker
The Dehydrator Cookbook
Waffles
The Coffee Book
The Bread Machine Cookbook
The Bread Machine Cookbook II
The Bread Machine Cookbook III
The Bread Machine Cookbook IV
The Sandwich Maker Cookbook
The Juicer Book
The Juicer Book II
Bread Baking (traditional), revised
The Kid's Cookbook, revised

Quick & Easy Pasta Recipes, revised
15-Minute Meals for 1 or 2
Recipes for the 9x13 Pan
Extra-Special Crockery Pot Recipes
Chocolate Cherry Tortes and Other Lowfat Delights
Lowfat American Favorites
Lowfat International Cuisine
The Hunk Cookbook
Now That's Italian!
Fabulous Fiber Cookery
Low Salt, Low Sugar, Low Fat Desserts
Healthy Cooking on the Run
Healthy Snacks for Kids

Creative Soups & Salads
Muffins, Nut Breads and More
The Barbecue Book
The Wok
Quiche & Soufflé Cookbook
Cooking for 1 or 2
New Ways to Enjoy Chicken
Favorite Seafood Recipes
No Salt, No Sugar, No Fat Cookbook
New International Fondue Cookbook
Favorite Cookie Recipes
Authentic Mexican Cooking
Fisherman's Wharf Cookbook
The Creative Lunch Box

Write or call for our free catalog.
Bristol Publishing Enterprises, Inc.
P.O. Box 1737, San Leandro, CA 94577
(800)346-4889; in California (510)895-4461